MothersWork

MothersWork

How a Young Mother Started a Business on a Shoestring and Built It into a Multi-Million Dollar Company

Rebecca Matthias

Currency

Doubleday

New York London Toronto Sydney Auckland

A Currency Book
PUBLISHED BY DOUBLEDAY
a division of Random House, Inc.
1540 Broadway, New York, New York 10036

Currency and Doubleday
are trademarks of Doubleday, a division of
Random House, Inc.

Library of Congress Cataloging-in-Publication Data

Matthias, Rebecca.
MothersWork: how a young mother started a business on a shoestring and built it into a multi-million dollar company.
Rebecca Matthias.
p. cm.
1. Mail-order business—United States. 2. Home-based businesses—United States. 3. Women-owned business enterprises—United States.
I. Title. II. Title: MothersWork.
[DNLM: 1. Businesswomen—United States.]
HF5466.M38 2000
658.8'72—DC21 99-19523
CIP

ISBN 0-385-49590-0

Printed in the United States of America
October 1999
First Edition
1 3 5 7 9 10 8 6 4 2

To my father and mother,

who taught me to believe in myself,

and to my husband, Dan,

who told me to reach for the stars

Acknowledgments

I would like to thank
my literary agent, Julie Castiglia,
and
my editor, Betsy Lerner,
two working mothers whom I admire enormously.
Without their help, I could not have written this book.

Contents

Contents

Contents

introduction

The Heart of an Entrepreneur

The name of my company is Mothers Work. I was twenty-eight years old when I started it, and I was pregnant. You've read a lot about men starting big technology companies in their garages. Well, I started Mothers Work in my front closet with $10,000 of savings.

Today I am the president of a $300-million public company with six hundred stores in malls around the country, and I have 3,500 employees reporting to me. And I am the mother of three wonderful children. I am asked to be on boards of corporations and universities, when it seems like only yesterday I was clueless and couldn't even read a balance sheet. I am the keynote speaker at events and conferences, when just the other day I was desperately seeking inspiration and guidance from those presentations myself.

I sell maternity clothes to mothers-to-be out of stores called Motherhood, Mimi Maternity, and A Pea in the Pod. The clothes are designed and manufactured in our headquarters facility in Philadelphia under those labels, each brand targeted to a different consumer segment and a different price point. Today Mothers Work, Inc., is the largest maternity clothing company in the country. Make that the world. No, make that the universe. I like saying that, because when I started my company, there were so many people who thought it was a dumb idea. People who thought I didn't have the slightest idea what I was doing. Many people were quick to offer the following wisdom when I described my dream: "If this were really such a good idea, someone would already have done it." Someone should have told that to Thomas Edison when he was inventing the electric lightbulb. I learned to trust my own instincts. I learned to try things, and when they didn't work to try other things.

You can do the same thing I did. You can start up a successful business and grow it. What you need to succeed lies within you. You just need to know how to harness your ideas and how to focus your energy. Like many women, it took me a long time to learn to value my ideas and, perhaps more important, my time. More women are responsible for start-up companies today than men. The Small Business Administration reported on their Web site in November 1998 that women are starting new firms at twice the rate of all other businesses and own nearly 40 percent of all firms in the United States. Furthermore, these 8 million firms owned by women employ 18.5 million people—one in every five U.S. workers—and contribute $2.3 trillion to the economy. But we still face age-old prejudices and misconceptions about our abilities and what the media want us to believe is good for our kids. In order to succeed in a start-up, we have to get rid of that acculturated conditioning of putting everyone else's needs ahead of our own. Only then can we focus our energy on our ideas enough to make them succeed.

Sometimes I look back and wonder how I ever ended up in business. I set out to be an architect and civil engineer, and I went on to obtain quite a few degrees in those subjects from major universities. But somehow the allure of starting a company proved to be a stronger siren call. When I was in high school, my father told me that if I wanted an interesting life I should start a company. I guess that idea stayed with me. I can certainly say that my life is interesting. On any given day I could be meeting investment bankers in New York, visiting stores in Denver, or reviewing dress designs on a fit model in our Philadelphia office. Or if it's not such a good week, I could be crisis managing a bad earnings report, or spending an entire weekend reading sales reports trying to figure out why sales are down, or making an emergency trip to a bank or a vendor when I was supposed to watch my daughter give a recital. And invariably, sometime around 1:30 A.M., I'm probably up worrying about next year's financial forecast, planning whom I can get to watch the kids while I'm gone next Wednesday night visiting stores, and thinking about recruiting for two key positions. In short, I'm having a ball.

I've learned a few things over the last eighteen years since I started my company about what works and what doesn't. If I had it to do all over again, I know just what I'd do differently. Just what I'd do exactly the same. And, of course, what I'd do better. In this book I'm going to share a few lessons from the front line. Doing business is like doing battle. And you have to be prepared to fight. This book will spell out the rules of starting a company. I will share some of the practical skills I've learned, such as how to raise money and how to write a business plan. How to find good people and how to keep them. I'll also give you some of the secrets of successfully starting a business while you're starting or raising a family at the same time.

One thing is certain: you must have the right frame of mind to start your own company. I've learned three simple rules to succeed in business, and if you follow them you will succeed: (1) think big, (2) focus, and (3) never give up. There. I've given you the essence of this book. I think all entrepreneurs who have followed these three rules have been successful. Actually, the biggest danger in starting a business is having a goal that's too small. When I started Mothers Work, I had a goal of having a successful mail-order catalog, with a fuzzy idea of how big the catalog might become. Over the years I learned that you only accomplish what you set out to achieve. In other words, if you plan to have a chain of 25 stores and you work hard, you might get there or you might not. But you will *definitely* not get to 50 stores, or 150 stores. My current goal, which was set three years ago, is to be $1 billion in revenue by the year 2005. I try to find time every week, maybe an hour on Saturday morning, or while I'm soaking in the bathtub, to visualize the future when I reach that goal. I think about what kind of managers I need to recruit, how many stores I'll have, what new business areas I'll be in. I'll definitely need a larger distribution facility. If you *see* the future, you'll know where you're going. Then it's just a matter of finding your way.

Focus is next. Think about sunlight pouring in through your window, warming the entire room. Now think about the same amount of sunlight going through a lens, focused into a tiny stream of intense heat, burning a hole through your dining room table. That's focus. We all have a finite amount of time, energy, and resources. The number of commitments we make determines how much time, energy, and resources are allocated to each one. So while I'm all for balance in life, I realize that it comes at a price—namely, a reduction in the focus put into any single commitment. Some people prefer a warm-room approach to life. By that I mean they spread their sunlight around to many aspects of their life. Starting a company may not be right for those people. I have found that the more you focus on your goal in business, the greater your success. The other parts of the room may come up cold, but you're going to burn a hole in the table. It all depends on what you want out of life.

Seventeen years after I started my company I can look back and realize that I got what I really wanted in life. I'm a mother with a business. I don't have a lot of friends. I don't have hobbies. I don't bake cookies for the class bake sales (my daughter has adjusted). I don't watch *Seinfeld*. I haven't gone to any of my class reunions. And there have been many consecutive years when I've skipped vacations altogether. I'm not what you would call well rounded. Just ask my mother. I have two focuses: my family and my business.

The "never give up" rule is probably the most obvious, and the hardest to do. You can only fail when you're no longer trying to succeed. But man, that's tough some days. I have a framed cartoon hanging on the wall next to my desk that shows a businessman pointing to one of those sales graphs with the line gyrating madly up and down but generally in an upward direction. He turns to his colleague and says, "I've learned not to worry." I can almost guarantee that the first thing you try will not work out. You have to keep trying new ways. Two steps forward, one step back. My initial idea of selling career maternity clothes through a mail-order catalog has metamorphosed so many times it is hardly recognizable. Every initiative had problems to work out. Some things worked, and some didn't. Believe me, there were lots of times when I would have *given* you my company if only you would have taken it. But if you stay with something long enough, things develop. You get a break. You figure out a better way. And you make a little more progress.

Think big. Focus. Never give up. That's your mantra. Everything else will fall into place. So whether you are just thinking about starting a company, or you're in the initial development stage, or you're ready to take your business to the next level, I'll try to give you the ammunition you need, in a step-by-step approach. Over the last seventeen years I have developed the business tools that have taken me from a four-page black-and-white catalog run out of my front closet to a public offering worth $19 million sponsored by some of the country's biggest investment bankers, and beyond. This is the story of how a new mom became a mom CEO. Take a break from all the giving and caring for others that you do, and give yourself a few hours to read this book and make your own plan for success. Believe in yourself. You can go as far as you think you can go. I'll help you every step of the way.

chapter one

Starting Up

Everything seems possible when you're twenty-eight. I was young, intelligent, ambitious. I had degrees from the best colleges. The year was 1981—the beginning of the decade of wealth and greed. I had just gotten married and I was helping my husband, Dan, with the Important Work of starting his computer company in Boston. The thing was, I didn't want to "help" someone. I wanted my own company.

Starting a company ranks right up there with great lifetime initiatives. It's like waving to your parents the day you go off to college. Like standing at the altar on your wedding day. Like setting off to discover the New World. Like Genghis Khan marching off to conquer Asia. It's a real high. I can see why some people start company after company. Even in the face of repeated failure, they try again and again. Every time it's a new beginning. Every business start-up could be the Big One. The new Bill Gates story. Look at Colonel Sanders. He was sixty-five when he started a little chicken restaurant. Do you see? It's *never* too late.

That's how I felt when I started Mothers Work. Like Christopher Columbus.

The other thing about starting a company is that anybody can do it. You don't have to get anyone's permission or send someone a résumé or pass a test. You might have a lot of experience before you start, or you might just take a flier and start a business on a hunch. Take me. I didn't know the first thing about clothes—maternity or otherwise. I also didn't know anything about mail-order catalogs, or fashion, or business in general. I did, however, have a stubborn ego-driven belief that I could run and even build a business. I thought I had a perfect product that no one else had thought of and that I was uniquely capable of understanding this market. I was convinced that I had discovered a true market void when I was pregnant and couldn't find a single article of clothing to wear to the office. And despite hearing that constant refrain, "If this were really such a great idea, someone else would have already done it," I ignored all naysayers and relied on my own gut instincts. I was perfectly qualified to start a business.

I think that entrepreneurs have a strange combination of impulsive, quick-decision-making ability and day-after-day-grind-it-out-and-refuse-to-quit stamina. For example, Dan and I were married about sixty days after we met, and we've been grinding it out ever since. Dan was starting up yet another computer company in Pennsylvania, and I was just out of graduate school, in my first job as a construction engineer, building a new addition to his plant. He says he fell in love with me when he saw me in those muddy boots and construction hat. I was attracted to his power and prestige. I knew almost immediately that I, too, wanted to be the president of a big company that I started and grew. The nice part was that he didn't think that was funny or impossible or even questionable. His only comment was "Why have you been wasting so much time in school when you could have started by now?"

Shortly after we met, I took Dan to my family's house for Thanksgiving, and we got married in January. Six months later we were relocated from Philadelphia to Boston so Dan could start computer company number 5 or 6 (who's counting?) with his friend from business school, with me "helping." I had finished up the construction project and was between assignments, trying to decide what to do next. The move to Boston had disrupted the next construction project I would have received. It seemed like the perfect time to try something new and become involved with a business start-up. But lacking any real business experience, I was relegated to the administrative side of things. All those excellent degrees I had in architecture and civil engineering that I had earned from the hotshot schools I went to were suddenly worthless. I was spending my days calling insurance agents and renting office furniture. My title was vice-president of administration. The "vice-president" part was clearly to humor me. As time passed, I did get pretty good at what I was doing, but it seemed like I was stuck in that administrative role, with no opportunity to break out into the real power positions. I worked my tail off researching and writing parts of the business plan, but when it came time to present it to venture capitalists, I was never invited to the meetings. I became more and more convinced that if I were ever going to be the president of a large company, it would have to be one I started.

Then I got pregnant.

It wasn't like it was unplanned. I mean, Dan was thirty-eight and he really wanted to get going with the fatherhood thing. I was only twenty-eight, but I was ready too (I thought)—even though few of my friends were even married yet, let alone pregnant.

I called my mother. Naturally she was thrilled.

"I think you should move back to Philadelphia," she said.

"Mom, we have a *business* here," I replied. "We can't just move."

"What could be more important than a baby?"

"What's that supposed to mean?" I asked. This was ridiculous. She didn't understand anything.

"Who's going to take care of it?"

"I am. What are you *talking* about?" I was starting to raise my voice.

"You," she snorted. "You're going to be working. You're going to need me to help you!"

"So I'll hire someone," I said. "How hard could it be?"

She thought about that for a minute. "I think you should move back to Philadelphia."

Of course time proved that she had the right idea. In the first place, I did need her to help me, and in the second, it was *very* hard, especially in those first few months. But while I was watching my pregnancy progress, everything still seemed possible. I had no idea what I was getting into.

Like most women do now, I worked right up to the day before my delivery. At the time, however, this was not only unusual, it seemed somehow immoral. Like I might hurt the baby. Somehow it meant I wasn't *serious* about being a new mother. Like I should be home putting up wallpaper in the baby's room.

During that time I also thought a lot about my future and what I wanted out of life. Working for Dan's computer company, I was learning a lot about business, but it was becoming clear that I was going to reach what is now called the glass ceiling. Dan and his partner had a lot more experience than I did in computers and computer start-ups. And as more and more bright young men were hired, I couldn't help but feel that I was being passed over. On the other hand, having the opportunity to be involved with a start-up opened my eyes to just how exciting it could be to create a new company out of nothing and help it grow. I questioned the value of all of my degrees in architecture and engineering. Had I just wasted my time all those years in school? As much as I loved construction and architecture, the allure of starting a business was beginning to take hold. Maybe I could combine the two by starting a business in the construction field. I was giving that some thought too.

Then there was the baby. How was I going to do anything at all when I had a baby to deal with? What a confused, mixed-up mess I was. As I went to work every day, all these thoughts were swirling around in my mind. And out of all this mental chaos, gradually a plan started to formulate. My pregnancy was the catalyst in my decision to change career direction, since everything else in my life was changing. I figured that I could spend some time at home with the baby while I got my business going. In the end I decided that the time was right to experiment and try my own hand at starting a business.

I was going to quit my job and start a business as soon as the baby was born. Something that I could run from our house—at least initially. I would spend time with the baby, then work while he/she slept, and maybe hire someone to fill in, taking care of the baby, a few hours a day so I could be really productive. That way, I could be the perfect mother, fulfill my career ambitions, and maybe even whip up a few dinner parties to help Dan's business at the same time.

How stupendously stupid and naive I was, weaving my little fantasy. Things turned out so differently. So much more complicated and difficult. Yet, my idea of combining a business and a baby *is* what got me to take the first step in my business. And once the ship was launched, I was pulled into a vortex of events spinning out of my control for many years after. Too stubborn to give up, and then too far into it to pull out, I *had* to make it work. And that, after all, is what makes new businesses survive. Never giving up.

While I was still pregnant, Dan and I would sit around our little kitchen table after work, brainstorming about my new business. An inveterate entrepreneur, Dan loved the idea of being involved in *two* start-ups at once, mine and his. He had fully supported my idea of quitting to start a new business.

"Why don't you start a new Green Stamp business? You know, like the one they used to have in the grocery stores. Customers collect Green Stamps that the grocery stores give them depending on how much food they buy. They lick 'em and stick 'em in these little books and then they trade them in for free gifts. The beauty part is that *the merchants pay you up front.* Then months later you redeem the stamps." He *loved* this idea. "It's *self*-financing." Now he was pacing back and forth across our little kitchen.

"I don't know," I said. "I don't know anything about that kind of business." (That was what I said about all his ideas.)

He stopped pacing and looked down at me. "Rebecca," he

said with a semipatient pained expression, "that doesn't matter. Do you think Rockefeller knew anything about oil before he started the Standard Oil Company?" I couldn't answer that one. "Do you think John R. Simplot knew anything about *french fries* before he patented the method of quick-freezing them and locked up the whole goddamn market in the *whole United States* for supplying french fries to everyone from McDonald's to Burger King to Long John Silver's?"

He couldn't believe how unimaginative I was. That patented french fry thing was one of his favorites. He shook his head. "All right," he said. "How about a mail-order business?"

How about a mail-order business?

"You can run it right from our house."

I was liking this.

"And you can have a national business right from the start. There's no limit to how big it can get. Look at Lillian Vernon. Look at that Horchow guy. They started from *nothing.*"

My father tried the mail-order business once, right after World War II. He bought a bunch of balloons wholesale and put an ad in the local paper for balloons. "BALLOONS," it read. "Kids love them."

It never really went anywhere, but he always talked about it. Anyone could start a mail-order business. I could do this. I could mail out catalogs and fill orders while the baby was sleeping.

"Okay," I said. "What would I sell?"

That question kept us busy for the next several weeks. How about a new kitchen product? How about a chess set for kids? How about a new kind of food-of-the-month club? How about a catalog of tools for women?

Meanwhile I was growing bigger and more pregnant every day. I was growing out of the navy-blue suit that had become my "uniform" in my role as vice-president of administration. Back then women were trying to get ahead by looking like men. *Serious* women wore man-tailored suits with little red foulard floppy bow ties on their crisp white shirts. I was certainly serious. My biggest problem became getting dressed in the morning once my zipper wouldn't go up anymore on my navy-blue skirt. And really, I didn't have time to be running around shopping. I was working my day job and starting a business at night.

I looked in the yellow pages under "Maternity." Interestingly enough, this could have been my first official act in starting my company. Later I came to regard the yellow pages as my "networking" handbook. Because everything I did that first year was something I knew nothing about and didn't have the slightest idea of whom to ask or where to go, I would start a sort of yellow-page chain. If I needed to find someone to print a catalog, I'd look up "Printers" and call one. The guy on the other end of the line would say, "Lady, we print industrial labels for the automotive industry."

I'd say, "Oh, well, do you know where I'd find a printer who prints catalogs?"

He'd recommend the printers' guild, which I learned has a list of all kinds of printers. Then I'd ask if he happened to have that number. And he'd say, "Sure. It's blippety-blop."

Then I'd call the printers' guild and they would give me a catalog printer's number, only he'd turn out to be a huge printer that didn't print anything less than 500 million catalogs at a time on something called a web printer, and he'd tell me for my size run I really needed a smaller sheet-fed printing plant, and why didn't I call Joe Blow over in Newton. And finally I'd call Joe Blow and he'd be the right one for me. I used to spend hours at a time on yellow-page chains.

So I looked up "Maternity Clothes" in the yellow pages and I found a bunch of them, and I figured I'd just drive on over to one of them at lunch the next day. They did seem to have cutesy names like "Storktime" and "Babylove," and stuff like that. Not like the places where I had been buying my power suits, not "Brooks Brothers."

It all became clear to me after I spent about five minutes in the first store. I walked right over to the salesperson and said, "Where are your suits?"

She motioned to the back and said, "You're going to love our selection. And we're having a sale today through Saturday. They start at $29.99."

As I walked to the back, I thought to myself, *$29.99? I must be in the wrong store. There's no way these can be any kind of quality suits.* I looked around in the back, but all I found were a bunch of polyester stretch pants and T-shirts with cute sayings like "Send Some More Pizza Down Here!" Oh, they'd love it if I walked into the office wearing that.

"Excuse me, miss," I said. "I can't seem to find your suits."

"They're right next to you." She pointed to a rack of bathing suits.

"Oh, no. I mean *suits*. Like a skirt and jacket. Preferably navy."

"Suits?"

Was I speaking the English language?

"You know, something to wear to *work.*" She was staring at me. I guess she finally looked at the power suit I was wearing.

"Well, dear," she said, "I don't think we have any *suits*. But we have some fabulous little dresses that would look very cute on you."

I didn't like the way she called them "little" and I certainly didn't want to look "cute." She led me up to the front of the store and proceeded to show me a collection of dresses that I can only say would be more appropriate for a ten-year-old than for my day off. The first one had a big white sailor collar and little puffs on the sleeves. It *was* navy blue, however, so I will give her that. The second one was little pink checks. It reminded me of the matching dresses my mother made for me and my two sisters when we were all under the age of ten. All it needed was the little straw hat to go with it. You get the drift. Did pregnant women actually wear these things? Did they suddenly revert into "cute" little girls to counterbalance the obvious statement their bodies were making: "I had sexual intercourse!" Was that going to happen to me? I started to panic. I started to sweat. Maybe I was having a hot flash. All of a sudden I didn't like the way this pregnancy experience was going.

"I don't think you have what I'm really looking for," I said, backing away from her. "Don't you know of any maternity stores that carry stuff to wear to work? You know, like *suits?*" I was trying to get one of those yellow-page chains going. But she just looked at me with that stare of hers. She obviously didn't have the slightest idea of what I was talking about.

I kept backing right out the door, mumbling my thanks under my breath as I left. I halfheartedly tried a couple of the other maternity stores on my list, but each visit was basically a repeat performance. I now had a big safety pin stretched across the top of the zipper in my skirt because I couldn't close it anymore. It was that night as we were dreaming up things to sell by mail order that the obvious product popped into my mind: career maternity clothes.

Dan loved the idea.

"This is good," he said. I suppressed my next thought ("I don't know anything about that business") and decided that sooner or later I had to just hold my nose and jump in.

There. I had a product. I was going to sell it through a mail-order catalog. I would start as soon as the baby was born. I had a plan.

I never did buy any maternity clothes. Since I was always on the thin side, I was able to improvise with regular clothes that were a size or two bigger than my normal size. I bought a gray jumper at Talbots that had a V-neck and buttoned down the front, and didn't have a waistband or a belt in the middle. I wore it with a white shirt and a red foulard floppy bow tie, and then put a navy-blue jacket on top, which I just left unbuttoned. It would have been nice to find a *navy* jumper that matched my navy jacket, so I could get that navy suit look, but that was asking a lot.

Thus my "maternity power suit" was born. It got me through all of my meetings while I was pregnant, and I spent the rest of my pregnancy planning my new business, while weaving my fantasy of life as a working mother, building a mail-order empire. All I can say is I had a few things to learn.

Isaac was born on November 2, 1981, at 4:00 A.M. I had been helping Dan negotiate a new bank deal that day, and we were at a critical juncture. So after being up all night in the labor and delivery room, Dan had to run home and shower and change and go back to work practically right after Isaac was born so he could resume negotiations. I was only sorry I couldn't go too. There I was sitting by myself in my hospital gown rereading the *Wall Street Journal,* as if something in its black, inky columns would tell me what to do now. Dan called me from the bank meeting a couple of times to ask me about some figure or some bank account. My body ached all over. And then out of nowhere the nurse would bring in this tiny baby and hand him to me like I was supposed to know what to do with him. I felt like I had one foot in the world of business and was halfway through the door into the world of motherhood. I was scared to death and I felt totally alone.

The next day Dan came and got me and Isaac and we headed home. My parents had flown up that morning to help out for a few days. I had stitches from the delivery and I had to sit on a big pillow in the car. Dan had the baby seat all ready, but it took us twenty minutes just to figure out how to work the safety belt. Then Isaac started to scream at the top of his little lungs, so we thought maybe he was hungry, and we took him out so I could nurse him a little. Then we had to start all over with the car seat. By the time we got to our house I was exhausted and my stitches hurt like hell. We walked in the front door and my mother was standing there with a big smile on her face. I could feel my composure give way. Tears were starting to well up. I wasn't normally the weepy type, but the combination of postpartum exhaustion, the fear of taking care of this tiny creature, and the hormonal roller coaster my body was on all got the best of me.

"Here," I said, and handed the baby over to my mother and went to bed. When I woke up, my mother had everything under control. I could smell pot roast cooking in the oven. The table was set, and the enormous mess I had left in the house before running to the hospital had been totally picked up and cleaned up. My mother had this little apron on and she was humming and whisking around doing things. Dan and my father were sitting in the living room sipping something and talking about airplanes or computers or something like that. My mother had spread out a big quilt on the floor and the baby was right there in the middle of everything, sleeping peacefully with a sunbeam peeking through the window and landing right on him. I felt like I had wandered into someone else's home by mistake. Maybe the Cleavers' or the Nelsons'. I could never keep this sort of thing going. I felt like I was going to cry again.

They all looked up at me.

"Hi," I said weakly.

My mother came up and gave me a little hug.

"Hello, little mother," she said.

Are you addressing me?

"Hey, you done good, Beck," my father said.

I didn't do anything. My body did.

"Can we eat now?" Dan said.

Finally, a useful comment.

Isaac opened his eyes and started to scream. Everyone started to laugh (except me).

"I guess he's hungry too!" my father joked.

Since I was nursing him, I was the only one who could do anything about it. Somehow I resented the fact that even though *I* was hungry and *I* was the patient, *I* had to stop and feed this screaming infant before I could feed myself. I had a long way to go in developing my maternal instincts. I was still waiting for my mother to take care of me. As I sat there nursing the baby, I started to calm down a little. Maybe I just had to get the hang of this Mother Thing. Isaac looked up at me and seemed to give me a little milky smile. Maybe things would be all right after all.

There was no going back. I was a mother now. In the months that followed, all the maternal instincts kicked in, especially a fierce desire to protect my baby. I could no sooner have given Isaac away than I could have given my own life away. In those same months my business would begin to overtake my life too. And like a child, it would latch onto me so completely that it would be part of me. I knew I would see it through. Though I wouldn't want to push the comparison too far, there are many similarities between having a child and growing a business. Anything you truly put your heart into will provide an inevitable stream of joy, frustration, disappointment, and then when you least expect it, growth and a completely new level of accomplishment. I was entering a whole new world. If you are a mother already, you probably have the better set of skills for running a business than most M.B.A.'s. And if you are starting a business, you will capitalize on those skills.

Where Ideas Come From and How to Test Them in the Marketplace

▼ ▼ ▼

A mail-order business is no different from any other business. It is all about selling a product to a customer. End of story. Everything else—the business cards, the office space, the computer accounting system, the catalog itself—is all an *expense*. Don't waste too much energy on beautiful stationery or a pretty office. Focus on selling a product and satisfying your customer, and you will have a successful business.

Therefore, the single most important step in creating your new business is your *product*, even if your product is a service and not a tangible item. Some of Wall Street's most successful investors choose the companies they invest in based on day-to-day contact with those companies' products. So, for example, if you love the new Campbell's beef stew that comes in the revolutionary pop-up container that can slide right into your microwave, you might think that company is really on its toes in understanding its customers' needs, and you might go out and buy a million or so shares of Campbell's. There is really no big mystery in a company's success. It comes from the customers who like the products and buy a lot of them.

Learn to think like a customer instead of a business owner, and you will have a direct link into the minds of your most important resource. If you like your product, other people may too. Don't make the mistake of trying to sell a product because it's easy to obtain, or it's cheap to make, or you have a lot of them, or you enjoy making them. None of these things matter if no one wants to buy that product. In 1981, when I started the Mothers Work catalog, my personal experience of shopping for maternity clothes to wear to work was so appalling that I just knew other women were going through the same frustration. The fact that I knew nothing about garments or catalogs was a minor problem compared to the major opportunity of the market void that I had discovered. I was my own best customer. I knew women were entering corporate life with a vengeance. I knew the number of women getting M.B.A.'s had skyrocketed, and I knew that these women were in the workforce to stay. Remember, if you have a product people want to buy, everything else can be figured out and solved.

One of my favorite examples of a business success story that reflects this philosophy is the Lillian Vernon catalog. Now a $258-million public company, Lillian Vernon started her mail-order empire by placing a single ad in *Seventeen* magazine for a personalized leather-embossed $1.99 belt and $2.99 bag. To this day she capitalizes on ordinary items that are personalized and sold by mail. Her genius is that she thinks like her customers and knows exactly what price they want to pay and for what items, with the added appeal of their own name on the product.

Think about your own experiences and needs. If you have specialized knowledge about a particular field or lifestyle, this could be a perfect opportunity to work in a niche market that larger companies are not interested in. Are you a fly fisherman? Maybe you know about special equipment and hard-to-find flies. The now famous Baby Jogger stroller was an example of two factors—the desire to jog and the need to parent—joining together into a new product that filled a vacuum. Likewise, the Jogbra, which was the brainchild of two women in their twenties, was based on their personal need for a firmer bra support when running. Four years after they started it they had sales of $1 million and had added other women's and men's sportswear items to their product line. Special religious needs? Dietary restrictions? Gardening knowledge? Hobbies? Ethnic groups with specific likes, tastes, or apparel? All of these situations could yield a niche market with unfulfilled product needs. You just have to uncover them through your ability to think like a customer and turn a market need into a business. Recently I saw a new product in a women's and girls' sports equipment catalog that made me say, "Why didn't I think of that?" It was a girl's baseball helmet with a special accommodation for ponytails. My ten-year-old daughter saw it and immediately wanted it. I would be willing to bet that that great idea was invented by personal necessity.

One advantage that I experienced in starting a mail-order business was that I immediately had a national market for my product. A mail-order business is not a corner store selling to a small group of people who happen to live in a given area. The benefit is that you can be successful with a product that appeals to only one out of one hundred people, because your total market is the entire 300 million or so people in the United States. Of course, the media you choose to advertise in will zero in on the right one out of one hundred people in each town. So mail order is great for products like left-handed golf clubs, advertised in the *National Golf Magazine*, $100 caviar, sent to mailing-list names obtained from *Gourmet* magazine, and, in my case, navy-blue maternity business suits, advertised in the *Wall Street Journal.* Products that wouldn't stand a chance in just any local mall.

Home party businesses, a la Tupperware parties, are another example of direct marketing that can start small and end up big. Lane Nemeth started a home party business called Discovery Toys in 1977 when she couldn't find the right educational toys for her two-year-old daughter. This working mother borrowed $5,000 and bought a selection of educational toys from existing suppliers, which she then sold at parties in her friends' homes. Her company now sells almost $100 million a year of educational toys, games, and books, still through direct-sales representatives. And of course, a discussion of direct sales would never be complete without mentioning Mary Kay Ash, founder of Mary Kay Cosmetics, also a working mother. Marketing her own skin-care line through home hostesses who conduct in-home beauty shows, she built a company that today sells over $1 billion annually.

There are many ways to market your products. Mail order

and home-based parties are just two examples. You may decide to retail your product in a store, or you may have a service business, a wholesale distribution business, or any number of other types of business. Whether you are inventing something new or simply marketing a group of hard-to-find products or adding a twist to an ordinary product, the key is in thinking like a customer and satisfying unmet demand. There are a million unserved market voids out there. Your job is to find just one!

Chapter One Checklist

- ▼ The single most important step in creating a new business is deciding on what your product is.
- ▼ Specialized knowledge about a field or lifestyle may suggest opportunities in a wide market.
- ▼ Look for a business that can start small and end up big.
- ▼ Learn to think like a customer, rather than a business owner.
- ▼ The key to success in any business is to satisfy customers' current demand.
- ▼ There are a million unserved market "voids." Your job is to find just one.

chapter two

My First Catalog

My parents left after a few days. My mother didn't really want to go, but my father said, "Oh, Wilma, leave the kids alone, for Chrissake." I think Dan was ready to reclaim his house, but I had mixed emotions. I knew that as soon as they left I would have to not only take care of Isaac all by myself but also face my new business start-up. No more procrastinating.

The next morning Dan drove off to work and I found myself seriously alone. I figured I'd spend the day planning my business. Working on a business plan. Getting a start on a catalog layout. Making some preliminary calls. Stuff like that. Isaac started to cry. Time to nurse.

After I fed him I put him in his crib. Then I had to take this little "sitz bath" for my stitches, which was basically sitting in a bucket of warm water for fifteen minutes. Then I made a cup of coffee and got a pencil and paper and sat at my desk. I wrote at the top: "Mothers Work." That's what I had decided to call my catalog. I sat there some more. Okay. Now what? I thought some more. Nothing came to me. I decided to call Dan. He was meeting with some venture capital investors, but he stepped out and took my call.

"What's up?" he asked.

I knew he was busy, so I got right to the point. "How do you think I should start?"

"Start what?" he asked.

"My *business.*"

He didn't say anything right away.

"Can we talk about this tonight? I'm right in the middle of something here."

Of *course* he was right in the middle of something. He already *had* a business. Couldn't he just take a minute and tell me how he did it?

"Okay sure no problem good-bye."

He could tell I was upset. "Why don't you start a list? Get organized. Figure out what you want to sell. Call some suppliers. Make a financial plan. Work on your written business plan. Then call around and—"

"All right!" I interrupted. "I can handle it!"

"See you tonight," he said.

I could hear Isaac crying in his room. It was ten o'clock and I hadn't even given him his bath yet. Now I was going to have to feed him first. I was running out of diapers too. I was definitely going to have to run to the drugstore. At least my mother had left me enough food in the refrigerator to scrounge up dinner. That would get me through one day.

By the time I got back to my paper and pencil it was four o'clock. I used to be able to buzz around and get things done so easily. Now even the simplest thing took forever. Just going to the drugstore required an amazing amount of setup. Stroller, diaper bag, baby wipes. In the car seat. Out of the car seat. And then practically every hour, nursing. There was just no letup. Exhausted, I decided to take a nap.

When Dan got home, I was an emotional wreck. The sum total of my day's work consisted of a piece of paper with the words "Mothers Work" written at the top.

"I don't think this is going to work out," I said. "I can't get anything done. And besides I don't know how to start anyway. Why don't I just hire a baby-sitter and go get a job?"

"You give up too easy," he said between bites of leftover mashed potatoes. "You just have to keep at it for a while. This is the fun part—starting up."

How could he call this fun? I had no idea what I was doing. I longed for the security of an established business. One where you knew what to do every day. Where there was a routine. People to work with. All I had was Isaac. I found myself talking things over with an infant. I didn't want a business anymore. I wanted a *job*.

"I think you need to get started on your catalog," he continued. "Get right into it and things will develop."

Things somehow did develop over the next few weeks. As I recuperated physically, I got my old energy back. And I learned how to get things done in spite of having an infant as my partner. I took the attitude "Where I go he goes." Which is actually the only attitude a nursing mother can take. I had this cheapy fold-up stroller which was really low-end compared to the Cadillac types of strollers most new mothers invested in. But the nice thing about it was it weighed about four pounds and I could carry it on my wrist like a pocketbook. I took it everywhere, and I wheeled Isaac around like a maniac everywhere I went. I'd stick a couple of diapers in my bag, and I was ready. No bottles or anything. Whenever he got hungry, I'd start nursing—no matter where I was or what I was doing. If there was a bathroom nearby, great; otherwise I'd be as discreet as possible. I didn't let the stares or the whispers bother me. I figured if there was a problem it was theirs. I nursed Isaac for six months without any bottles or food supplements, and for that time we were like a team, as if an invisible string attached us from his little body to mine, and we could never be separated. I was definitely starting to get the hang of that Maternal Thing.

In order to get my catalog started, I figured I needed three things: inventory; the catalog itself; and advertisements to solicit customers. I tackled the inventory first. I had the advantage of having been a customer, so I felt that I knew what would sell. Over the years, as my business grew, I never stopped thinking of my business as if I were the customer. I try not to think, "Will they buy this?" Instead, I ask myself, "Would *I* buy this?" The most obvious product need was for a navy-blue suit. Next I would find a crisp white shirt. Then I would round out the assortment with other suits, shirts, and dresses. Real dresses that you would wear to the office, not those infantile ones that I had seen in the local maternity stores.

After some initial research and yellow-page chains, I made a few contacts with wholesale maternity clothes manufacturers on Seventh Avenue in New York. I made an appointment to see them, and next thing I knew I was on the Delta shuttle to

La Guardia Airport with Isaac, six weeks old, and my fold-up stroller. I wheeled him right down the aisle, sat down, and nursed him to sleep. So far so good.

I found a cab at La Guardia, and we were off to the city. It felt great to be on a business trip. I was on a mission. I had a purpose. I knew exactly what needed to get done, and I was making real progress. I would have carried my power briefcase, but I was out of hands, between my fold-up stroller, diaper bag, and pocketbook. Oh well. I would just have to exude confidence and power.

My first appointment was with Betty Bailey, of the Betty Bailey Maternity Showroom, which featured five lines of "upscale" maternity brands. Her showroom was on the fifth floor of 1400 Broadway, a building right in the middle of the garment district of Manhattan. I was nearly run over by a rolling rack filled with dresses being pushed right up the middle of the street as I got out of the cab.

Betty herself was seated at the front desk as I walked in. She was a trim blonde in her fifties. She had on a tailored suit, with matching shoes, and her hair was perfectly coiffed. I felt relieved to be working with such a professional-looking woman. Surely she would understand what I was looking for.

She buzzed me in and, hardly looking up from her papers, she waved me into the showroom. "Just go ahead in. I'll be there in a minute," she said.

I guess I wasn't exactly her highest-priority customer.

I went into a cramped room filled with racks of clothes and a couple of wire grids in the middle to display garments. I sat down at a little table that had a bowl of miniature Hershey bars and another bowl of sharpened pencils that said "Betty Bailey Maternity Showroom" on them. Isaac was sitting in his little stroller, all slumped over, the way he did in the cheapy stroller. Betty made me wait for what seemed like a very long time. Finally she breezed in and sat down across from me.

"So what can I show you?" she asked, all bright and chipper, in a sort of patronizing way. She didn't even acknowledge Isaac's presence.

"Well, I'm going to start a mail-order catalog for career maternity clothes," I started. "I'm looking for suits and dresses that could be worn to the office. Normal clothes. Not like most of those typical maternity clothes. When I was pregnant, I had such a hard time finding professional-looking clothes."

She glanced at Isaac, then back at me. I could see her roll her eyes slightly.

"You know, every pregnant girl wants to come in here and start a maternity business," she said. "There are already plenty of maternity stores out there. What makes you think you're going to do anything different?"

I wasn't really ready for such a question. I guess I should have been more diplomatic talking about those "typical maternity clothes."

"What I mean is I want to specialize in more 'upscale' clothes," I said, trying to backtrack and get on her good side. "I was thinking you might have *better* maternity clothes than the ones I saw when I was pregnant."

"Dear, I carry *only* the better lines," she said in an irritated tone of voice.

I latched onto this right away. "Could you show me some of your *better* dresses and suits?"

She hopped up and began pulling things off the racks and hanging them on the wire grids. I had to admit, some of the things she was hanging up were a lot better than the polyester pants and cute Ts I had seen when I was pregnant. She had a few reasonable dresses and some tailored pants. What she didn't have was anything that even *resembled* a navy-blue power suit, or even any suit at all.

"How about that navy dress?" I asked. "The one with the red bow. How much does that cost?"

She looked at the ticket hanging from the neck. "It wholesales for $69.90."

I mentally doubled the number. I knew from reading a book on retailing that the retail price was supposed to be twice the wholesale cost. A dress for $140.00 was what I was looking for.

"How many of a style were you planning to buy?" she asked.

I was trying to figure out an answer to that question when her phone rang. I could hear her assistant answering it in the next room.

"Betty!" she screamed. *"It's Saks on the phone."*

Betty seemed to jump to attention. She straightened out her skirt and touched her hair into place. "You can look through this and call me later," she said over her shoulder as she left the room to take the call.

I had never been given such a quick brush-off in my life. You'd think she'd want to cultivate a new customer, for crying out loud. You'd think she'd have the *decency* to shake hands before she dumped me for Saks. You'd think she'd want to give Isaac a little hug. Something. I didn't quite know what to do next. I was trying to gather my thoughts when Isaac started to cry. He had gradually slumped farther and farther into his little stroller so that he was now just a little ball in the seat. I knew that tone of voice. He was getting ready to crank into a major scream. I quickly scooped him up, grabbed his stroller, and started out the door before we made a scene. As always, we were on the same wavelength. When he was hungry, I was filled with milk. My breasts were starting to leak and the nursing pads I had in were saturated. I could feel the front of my blouse developing a big milk mess.

"Is there a ladies' room nearby?" I asked Betty's assistant, trying to keep the panic out of my voice.

She handed me a key on a ring with a huge plastic *B* on it. "Down the hall, past the elevator, and on your right."

As soon as I closed the door, I tore down the hall and into the bathroom, Isaac getting louder by the second. It was tiny and dingy without any place to sit down. I leaned against the corner of the sink and fed him. There was really no place to lay him down to change his diaper, so I took my jacket off and laid it on the dirty tiles and changed him right there. *(Please, please, don't pee on my jacket.)*

By now I was late for my next appointment, so I threw Isaac into the stroller and ran back up to Betty's showroom to return the big *B* key and then back down to the elevator, pushing the little stroller like a madwoman. By the time I got to the next showroom I must have looked deranged. My jacket was filthy, half on, half off; I had milk stains all down my blouse, and I was panting and out of breath. The receptionist looked at me with an expression that said, "Don't come any closer or I'll scream."

I paused to get my breath and told her that I was a few minutes late for my appointment and would she *please* inform Mr. Kent that I was here because I knew he was waiting for me. You know, trying to get back in control of the situation.

She motioned me into the showroom and I collapsed into a chair at one of the tables and immediately dove into the little jar of M&M's. Thank God for this candy thing that every showroom seemed to have, because by now I was starved and light-headed since I hadn't eaten since 6:00 A.M. And if I didn't get something to drink soon, I was going to pass out from dehydration. Nursing required a constant intake of fluids.

Isaac was a little fussy since I hadn't even had time to burp him after the bathroom feeding, so I picked him up and started patting him just as Mr. Kent walked into the room. At that moment Isaac let out a huge belch and spewed sour milk all over the carpet in front of Mr. Kent's feet.

It's times like these when you really get to know a person. I mean there I was, a truly pathetic individual, clearly in need of understanding and compassion. And there he was, holding the power in his hands to either make me feel like a worthless worm or lift me up and rebuild my self-confidence. In the case of Mr. Kent, he turned out to be a true prince. He got this big grin on his face and said, "How'd you train that kid to throw up on cue like that?"

I smiled back at him. "Do you think I could get a glass of water?"

We hit it off right away and he turned out to be an incredibly good source of information about maternity clothes. Even though his lines weren't exactly what I was looking for, I found a few things to order from him, and we were friends for many years after.

I slogged through the rest of the day's appointments. By the time I got on the plane to go home, my head was pounding and my back was killing me. Isaac was a trooper. He slept all the way home, and the woman sitting next to me on the plane said how lucky I was to have such a good baby. My trip had mixed results. On the one hand, I had found some good-quality merchandise to put into my catalog. But the hard-core career clothing I was looking for just didn't seem to exist. It was as if an entire segment of the clothing industry had been excluded from the maternity world. There was no maternity navy-blue power suit. Period. I now understood why none of the maternity stores carried career clothing. There was none being manufactured.

I didn't get home until around eight that night. I was ravenous. Dan was waiting with pizza in the oven when I got there. It was a little dried-up but it tasted delicious. I told him all about my trip while I nursed Isaac in one arm and shoveled pizza in my mouth with the other. The good news was that I was more sure than ever that there was a void in the market that needed to be addressed. The problem was I didn't know how to go about filling it.

"What exactly do you want to put in the catalog that you can't find?" he asked as he handed me another slice of pizza.

I thought about my own experience of going to work and being pregnant. "If I could have had my 'maternity power suit' in matching navy blue, instead of a gray jumper and navy jacket, that would have been the perfect outfit," I said. "I didn't see anything even resembling that today."

"Okay," he said. "If you're so sure there's a market for your maternity suit, why don't you just mock something up in the catalog and see if anyone buys it."

"Mock something up? How do I do that? This isn't the computer industry. I can't just go make a cardboard model and photograph it. I can't just . . ."

"Can't, can't, can't," he mimicked. "Can't never could. Why don't you get creative?"

"Okay, let's say I figure out a way to mock one up and photograph it. What happens if someone orders one?"

"Then you'd know it was a good product. That's the whole *idea,*" he said.

"Yeah, but I wouldn't be able to fill that order. It would be like bad-faith advertising. And besides, I'd lose that revenue opportunity. Because I'd take up a part of the catalog with something I didn't have to sell." *Can't, can't, can't.*

"Well," he said slowly, "then you'd just have to make it."

I looked at him. All I could think was *I don't know anything about that business.* I had to stop thinking that way. I had to be braver. If he thought I could do it, then maybe I could. Besides, what did I have to lose? I could always go get a job. I had degrees. I was young.

"Okay," I said. "Okay. I can do that."

That was how I got into manufacturing.

Mocking up the maternity suit turned out to be relatively easy. I went back to Talbots and bought a new gray jumper. (Mine had been worn so many times it was ready for the thrift shop.) I went to Jaeger and bought a new navy jacket. Next I bought some Rit dye. Then I took it all to the laundry room and started dying the jumper darker and darker. I had a Polaroid camera, so I could check out the shade in a photograph until I got it right. I had already decided that the first catalog was going to be black and white, to save money, so I only had to get the shades of the jacket and jumper to be the same grayish tone in a black-and-white photograph. Even though the jumper was actually gray, I was going to describe the outfit as a "navy suit."

The second component of my business was the production of the catalog itself. I had given myself a total budget of $10,000, and so far I had spent about $3,500 for the inventory, including all the things I had bought in the showrooms, as well as the navy-blue suit. I figured on another $3,500 for the catalog itself, and maybe $3,000 for advertising. Putting together all the ingredients of a catalog involved one long yellow-page chain. The photographer led me to the graphic artist. I found models from a local modeling school. Every decision was an education. What kind of paper should the catalog be on? Slick? Glossy? Matte? How many pounds, what shade of white? I learned how to turn each question back around to the supplier. For example, I found that if I just said, "What do you recommend?," he'd usually reply, "Well, it depends what you're looking for, and how much you want to spend, and what the specific catalog is for, and blah blah blah." But if I just said, "If it were your business, what would *you* choose?," he'd say, "Well, I'd probably pick White Corolla paper #504." Then I'd say, "Okay, that's what I'm going to use."

We did the photo shoot on a nasty, freezing, rainy Saturday in March. I had gotten one of the lawyers who represented Dan's computer company to let me use his office on the weekend. I wanted to do the photography in a professional office setting. In hindsight this was a really lousy idea, because it's much harder to control the outcome if you're not in a photographer's studio. The lighting is never just right, and you have to keep setting up the camera and trying different film to see which is right for those conditions, and you never really get the ideal background because the furniture isn't exactly in the right place, and so forth. I should have listened to the photographer. But somehow we got through the day. I only wanted to pay the models for one day, because I was on such a tight budget, so we were under a lot of pressure to get all the shots done. I also had to get the showroom samples back by FedEx right away. I had to practically get down on my hands and knees and beg Betty to lend me four goddamn dresses for one stupid day so I could photograph them. You'd think she'd pay *me* for the opportunity to have them in my catalog. She wasn't exactly a believer in my success. On top of that, Isaac had a cold, and he wasn't his usual easygoing self. I had to keep nursing him and holding him while I ran around straightening the wrinkles from the models' clothes before every shot, and putting little props in their hands, like a lawbook, or a pencil and legal pad. Dan was the advance man. He would stay one shot ahead, looking for a new vantage point to get a new look, and then he and the photographer would lug all the lights and equipment to the next area.

We finished up by about seven. I was so worn-out I could hardly move. We went to Friendly's for dinner, and while I packed in an extra-thick chocolate milk shake and two cheeseburgers (nursing mothers eat a lot) I wondered for the fifty-ninth time what I was doing and if I would ever get anywhere. And for the fifty-ninth time Dan told me to keep going and not give up. We went home and I collapsed into bed.

I only had $3,000 left in my budget for advertising. My idea was to run small space advertisements in newspapers and magazines for the catalog itself. I was planning to charge $2 for the catalog to sort out the lookers from the buyers, mostly because I didn't have enough money to print very many catalogs. Then I was planning to include a little swatch card of the fabrics in the catalogs. That way, even though the catalog was black and white, my customers would be able to see the actual fabrics the clothes were made of, which I reasoned would be even better than a color picture. Besides, four-color printing costs were staggering compared to black and white. Of course, the actual process of getting a couple of measly yards of fabric to make into swatches was like pulling teeth. You can imagine how Betty felt about it. After all, I was only ordering twenty units per style, which I'm sure was peanuts compared to the Saks Fifth Avenue orders.

In the end I could only afford two advertisements, one in the *Wall Street Journal* and one in the *New Yorker.* They ran only once. Each was about one inch high and three inches wide, and it screamed "PREGNANT?" across the whole top half of the ad. Then the bottom half said where to write for the catalog of maternity clothes for pregnant executives. I didn't even have an 800 toll-free number or any telephone number at all.

I figured the "PREGNANT?" would stand out in the *Wall Street Journal,* which surely every pregnant executive read. I don't know if the *New Yorker* was the best second choice, but I was going for the sophisticated mail-order buyer and I knew that every doctor's office waiting room had one and that they are always chock-full of mail-order ads.

I remember the day the ad hit the *Wall Street Journal.* I was incredibly lucky with the placement, because in such a big paper it could have been totally lost. It ran right next to the continuation of a front-page article on the Patty Hearst kidnapping, which was a really interesting story as well as having terrific appeal to women.

Things were getting exciting now. All my hard work was

coming together. I had rented a post-office box to receive the catalog requests, and I started each day by driving over to see what I got, hoping and praying for a big haul. The first letter was exhilarating.

"Please send me your catalog for pregnant executives," it said. "Sharon Beasley, 5600 Oak Street, Chicago, Ill." What a moment. I was in business. She sent a check for $2. *My first revenue.* She had seen my ad, and she wanted my products. I love you, Sharon. I taped the letter above my desk.

Over the next few weeks the catalog requests built up to a steady fifteen or twenty each day. Every catalog request required a swatch card. At night after dinner, our kitchen became a swatch card manufacturing center. I had printed up little cards with places for each one-by-two-inch fabric swatch. After much discussion, I had decided to staple the fabric on, rather than glue it, so my customers could really get the feel of the fabric. The first hundred or so were individually cut by me with pinking shears so the edges wouldn't fray. Then Dan would staple them to the cards. By the end of the evening my hands would ache, and poor Dan stapled his fingers once or twice. Later we advanced our technology when I located a paper cutter that had a serrated edge, and an industrial strength stapler. As we cut and stapled, we'd discuss my progress.

In some ways the biggest step was behind me—starting. Going from the talking stage to the doing stage. Testing your idea by trying to sell a product. Not analyzing the market or forming a focus group or writing a business plan. Just going out there with a product and asking someone to buy it. Now I was going to find out if they would.

The Nuts and Bolts of Launching a Mail-Order Business

▼ ▼ ▼

Okay, so you have a great idea. Now, what is the best method of getting your product to your customer? I took the straightforward way. I bought a lot of clothes, photographed them, printed them into a catalog, and advertised in consumer publications. There are definitely many consultants who could design and print a catalog for you, and would almost certainly do a better job, but I think you should seriously consider doing it yourself. Get used to doing things you've never done before. You will learn a lot more about the process. It will be a crash course, and the knowledge you gain will be even more valuable than the money you save. No one will bullshit you in the future about costs, expertise, or anything else.

Before you do anything, get ahold of twenty or thirty catalogs and sort through them until you find a couple you want to use as a model for your own (i.e., copy them). There is nothing wrong with this! If imitation is the highest form of flattery, then I have complimented some of the best. When you have some idea of the direction you want to take, I suggest you start by finding a graphic artist. (You guessed it—check the yellow pages.) He or she will help you find all your other professionals, including a photographer and a printer. She'll also help you get started with basic things like a logo, letterhead, and any other graphics you need. A graphic designer will also lay out the catalog and help you with all the typesetting, which includes selecting the style of type and getting the words on the paper.

When I produced my catalog, I had the help of a friend who was a writer. He helped me with some of the copywriting, including product descriptions. On subsequent catalogs, I did this myself. It really isn't hard. I used to liberally steal great copy from other catalogs I liked. Sales lines such as "our best-selling slim-leg style pant, now in a soft, stretch twill for an exceptionally comfortable fit" could be lifted right out of almost any apparel catalog with a few minor changes to accommodate my product.

Once you have your catalog all laid out, you are ready to photograph. Of course you will be your own artistic director. Everything from the background to the props you use, as well as the overall look, should be planned out before the photo shoot. Again, I advise you on your first try to find a few catalogs you like, and re-create their look in your own style.

Printing the catalog is a simple matter. The type of paper you use, the quantity you print, and other details need to be worked out with your printer. There are print brokers who, for a fee, will find the best and most appropriate printer for you, and then monitor the process, including tweaking the color as it comes off the press. But you don't need one! Get three bids from printers and go with the best one. When I printed my first catalog, I made the mistake of printing too few to save a few hundred dollars in the short run. Once you set the presses up, the printing of each additional thousand catalogs is cheap. When I ran out of catalogs, I had to set the presses up all over again and spend much more money to get that extra thousand printed. Believe me, this was not the only mistake I made during this process, but as long as you keep picking yourself up from the floor, you can recover from every mistake.

Depending on the type of product you are selling, you may want to distribute your catalog (1) by advertising in magazines and newspapers with a telephone number to call or a mailing address or (2) by renting one or more mailing lists and sending your catalogs out unsolicited or (3) over the Internet. In my case, there were no lists of three-months-pregnant women. By the time their names could be collected and made available to rent on a list, they were well beyond the time they would buy maternity clothes by mail. So I was forced to do a three-step program of advertising the catalog, then sending the catalog, then converting those catalog requests into customers. Of course a smaller way to test your mail-order idea would be to have a single product, skip the catalog completely, and just advertise your product in a space ad. A great twenty-dollar product can be a huge success in its own right. Like the fabulous Triple Edge car window wiper, which was invented by two women. They had a huge business and they never had to print a catalog.

Your choice of media will probably be obvious to you based on the audience you are targeting. You want to focus on the cost per thousand readers, not the absolute cost. For example, if you are selling to lawyers, the local bar association publication might sell a quarter page for $500 and have a circulation of 2,000, whereas the national counterpart might sell a quarter page for $2,000 and have a circulation of 100,000. Don't cheap out here. The cost per thousand readers is $250 in the local publication and $20 in the national one. Always look at cost per thousand when you examine your media choices.

Make sure you put a unique code in the response address for every advertisement, and when your customer calls or writes, figure out a way to capture that code and analyze how each ad performed, both in generating catalog requests and in sales. That way you'll know where to put your ad dollars next time. If you're using a computer to track sales, this will be simple.

As you develop your business, your customer list will be your most valuable asset. Make sure you have a way to collect as much information as possible about all of your customers. In my case, because I only had my customer for the duration of her pregnancy, I had to constantly generate new names, and I couldn't build a "repeat customer" business. This proved to be one of the fatal flaws in my whole mail-order concept and ultimately pushed me into opening stores.

If you decide to rent a mailing list to send out your catalog, you need to get hold of a list broker. I suggest you contact the Direct Marketing Association and get their magazine, in which many list brokers advertise. You can reach them on the Web at *www.the-dma.org* or write to them at 1120 Avenue of the Americas, New York NY 10036-6700. You should also contact the National Mail Order Association at 2807 Polk St. NE, Minneapolis MN 55418-2954, or Web site *www.nmoa.org/Library/webtips.htm.* Your list broker will help you find the right list for your targeted audience. Whether it is another catalog's house list or a conglomeration of names with certain demographic or consumer attributes compiled from many lists, you can rent names on a onetime basis for anywhere from $25 per thousand to $125 per thousand. They will come either on preprinted mailing labels or a computer tape. Once you get a response from one of these rented names, that customer belongs on your list. A successful response rate is somewhere between 1 and 3 percent of all names mailed out.

The Internet is the wave of the future. We all know that. If you think your product would benefit by being marketed on the Internet, you will be somewhat of a trailblazer. We have only recently gone onto the Web with an on-line catalog. So far we have had modest but growing results. Without going into very much detail here, I will say that visibility of your product on the Net is the key to its success. The various search engines all need to be covered, and it is important to be listed near the top of your category to be found by your customer. Other than that, I am also learning how to harness this new marketing tool and I am counting on making many mistakes before I get it right!

Mail order is a great way to market a specialty item that has a narrow customer base but national appeal. You can reach a large audience with a minimal investment. And since a mail-order business can be started and run from the home, it can be a perfect solution for women with small children who are looking for a home-based business. Anyone can start a mail-order business. As in any new business, success will come from identifying a product that is unique and addresses a market need. Of course the next challenge you face will be sourcing that product. It's one thing to have an idea and market it. It's another to deliver a product to a customer. I found out just how challenging that could be early in my business career.

Chapter Two Checklist

▾ Anyone can start a mail-order business—and since it can be run from the home, it can be a perfect solution to women with small children looking for a home-based business.

▾ Get used to doing things you have never done before. The knowledge you'll gain will be more valuable than the money you'll save.

▾ In creating a catalog, copy liberally from other catalogs you like.

▾ Once the presses are set up, each additional thousand catalogs are cheap. Don't pinch pennies by printing too few.

▾ In advertising, focus on the cost per thousand readers, not the absolute cost.

▾ Make sure you have a unique code in the response address for every advertisement so you'll know where to put your ad dollars next time.

▾ Collect as much information as possible about your customers.

▼ To rent a mailing list, you'll need a list broker. Contact the Direct Marketing Association and the National Mail Order Association.

▼ The Internet is the wave of the future—but visibility of your product on the Net is key.

chapter three

If You Build It, They Will Buy It

One of my first suppliers, a seasoned manufacturer who had been making maternity clothes for about fifty years, told me, "Retailing isn't complicated. You buy for five dollars and sell for ten dollars. You don't have to go to Harvard Business School to learn that." Essentially he was right. But my business became somewhat more complicated right off the bat because of that damned navy-blue suit that I had mocked up in the catalog. When my first order came for the suit, I became a manufacturer as well as a retailer. Today Mothers Work is almost completely vertically integrated; that is, we design, manufacture, and then retail our product. It's the same way The Gap works. When you go into a Gap store, all the labels on the clothes say "The Gap." They are all produced by The Gap, and you can buy those products only in Gap stores. Contrast that with, say, Macy's. You go into

Macy's, and you find all kinds of different labels. Everything from Calvin Klein to Revlon to Liz Claiborne. Macy's didn't make any of it. They bought it from lots of different manufacturers. All they do is retail (buy it for five and sell it for ten). So the final consumer price has two profit layers in it—one for Liz Claiborne and one for Macy's. The advantage of being vertically integrated is that you cut out the middleman and the profit he would have made. In theory, either The Gap can sell their khaki pants for a lower price than Macy's, with the same profit as Macy's, or they can price them the same as Macy's and make a bigger profit.

Of course I hadn't thought any of this through. I was merely trying to get the right product into my catalog. At first, that mostly meant buying for five and selling for ten. I credit the navy-blue suit for taking me in a whole different direction. Now that I had a catalog, the next step in my education involved filling the orders. Up until now everything I had done was about spending money. A business is about *making* money. And that's where the suit comes in. When that first order came through, I felt a mixture of excitement and fear. I knew I was going to have to figure out how to make the suit and fill the order—after all, it was for $250, the most expensive item in the catalog.

I couldn't get anything done that day because I really wanted to talk it over with Dan, and I was trying to restrain myself from calling him over every little thing. As usual, when he got home that evening, I didn't even let him get his jacket off or ask how his day was before I launched into my latest development. Dan took it all in stride and was immediately ready to discuss my new manufacturing business.

"You've got to reverse-engineer your own suit. Then you'll know how to make it," he said matter-of-factly.

"Dan, this is a suit, not a Boeing 707."

"Doesn't matter. It's the same process. Go get your old suit and let's look at it."

I pulled my suit out of the closet and we laid it on the living room floor and studied it from every angle. Two engineers in our laboratory, we looked like we were about to invent nuclear fusion. I had Isaac in his little plastic baby chair right in the middle of everything. We sliced the jacket lining open to see what was inside. We made a list of all the components: buttons, labels, lining, thread. I had done a little sewing when I was in high school, so I had some idea about what I was looking at. I took notes. Basically we decided that I needed three things: materials, a pattern, and someone to sew it all together.

The next day Isaac and I drove into downtown Boston to a fabric store with my materials list. I told the store clerk I was making my husband a suit and I wanted the *best* wool suiting he had. He sold me five yards of a navy gabardine. Dan and I had looked at all the suits in his closet so I could determine the right kind of power suit fabric. In the end I chose the gabardine because it resembled the fabric in Dan's navy blazer. It cost $20 per yard. When you added in the buttons, lining, and other components, I spent about $115. By the time I paid someone to make a pattern and sew this thing, I was going to be lucky if I made any money at all.

"Don't worry," Dan said. "This is just a prototype. You can worry about making money later. Just get a good product."

Just get a good product. That was my mission. Once again, I consulted the yellow pages. No patternmakers listed. Okay. How about "sewing contractors"? Forget it. I tried a few tailors and quickly found out that they didn't make patterns and that they would charge upwards of $200 to make a suit. I put this information in the back of my mind in case I got really desperate. Time was of the essence. This lady wasn't going to wait around forever for me to fill her order. I figured I had two, maybe three weeks to pull this thing off. And unless I actually delivered a product, I wasn't really going to know if my idea was any good. Anybody could order from a picture. But would she actually like the real thing?

I wasted the whole day making calls and looking through the yellow pages. When Dan came home, I was panicking again.

"This isn't working. There are no sewing contractors in Boston."

He threw his briefcase on the couch and looked at me, assessing the situation.

"Why don't we go to Friendly's for dinner?" he said. "I'm starved."

It was obvious that I was in no state of mind to think about making dinner. I grabbed Isaac, and twenty minutes later we were eating burgers at Friendly's.

"This isn't going to work," I said. "This damned suit is going to cost more to make than the price I listed it at, and besides, I have no idea how to get it made. I'm running out of time and I wasted the whole damned day on it."

"Why don't you go to New York? They must have sewing contractors there."

"I don't have time for that," I said. "Besides, I can't keep running to New York every time I get one single order."

"How about a school of design? Why don't you get a student from a design school to make it for you?"

"Dan, they don't *have* any design schools in Boston."

He was pushing the food around on his plate, kind of distracted. Like he wasn't even thinking about how to get this suit made. Suddenly he put his fork down and looked up.

"How would you feel if I sold my part of the computer business and retired?"

Just like that. I guess it wasn't a total surprise. If I hadn't been so busy whining about my business and my problems, I might have heard that he wasn't exactly thrilled about the way things were going with his partner. I did have a fleeting twinge of uneasiness about our financial future. I mean *someone* around here had to be gainfully employed. On the other hand, shouldn't Dan have the right to pursue his dreams too? Why should he have to shoulder all the financial burden? The way things were going, though, it didn't seem highly likely that Mothers Work would put Isaac through nursery school, let alone through college. At that time, the catalog was in the infant stage too. Based on the initial results, although there was a lot of interest in the catalog, the number of orders was tiny. I had no idea whether I even had a viable business or not. I knew that Dan would make a lot of money when he sold his business, but it wouldn't be enough to live on for the rest of our lives. As I grappled with this new development, Dan just looked at me, waiting for me to say something.

"Well," I said, "what are you going to do after you retire? You're only thirty-nine. Don't you think that's a little young to retire?"

"I was thinking I would write a novel. Do something entirely different. While we're young. I'm so tired of computer chips, I never want to see another one as long as I live. At least not for a long time. Either you'll make a ton of money selling maternity clothes, or I'll sell my novel and make millions. Then there's the movie after that."

He was back on his cheeseburger now. He had our future figured out. Somehow I didn't have a lot of faith in either scenario. I was starting to get a stomachache.

"Dan, you've never written a novel," I pointed out.

He gave me that patient but exasperated look.

"So what?"

Silly me. Dan didn't go by most people's rules that said you could only do what you have done before. He felt that he could do whatever he put his mind to. He thought I could too. We finished our cheeseburgers and went home. I figured I'd find a way to make the suit, one way or another.

The next day I expanded my search. I went to the library and got out the yellow pages for all the neighboring towns around Boston. Boston isn't like most cities that have a huge metropolitan reach. It's really a cluster of little cities. Weston, Lexington, Burlington, Newton. They're all a stone's throw from downtown, but they're all separate cities, and each one has its own yellow pages. I finally located a sample maker in Lowell, Massachusetts. It was a two-hour drive, but Isaac and I made our way there that afternoon with my materials and my old suit. The moment I walked in I knew that this was what I had been looking for. The sample maker was in a strip center, in what probably used to be a Payless Shoe store or something. About ten ladies wearing brightly printed smocks were sewing on industrial-looking machines. They all looked up and smiled at Isaac, who was sleeping in his stroller. The owner was a Portuguese man who was cutting up long pieces of fabric with what looked like a big round electric saw. The noise was a little deafening with all that equipment going at once. He seemed to get it right away when I explained what I wanted. I gave him my old suit to work from and my navy fabric, and he said he'd make a size 8 pattern and one sample garment.

"Why don't you add about three or four inches to the waistline so it will fit her if she gets bigger than I was," I said.

"What kind of interlining do you want me to use?" he asked. "And do you want sleeve heads in the jacket?"

Since I had no idea what interlining or sleeve heads were, I fell back on usual tactics.

"Just use whatever you think will work best."

He charged me $65 for the whole thing, and he told me it would be ready in one week. When I picked the suit up one week later, I couldn't believe my eyes. It was exactly what I had in my mind when I started the whole business: a matching navy-blue maternity power suit. I felt so proud of myself. I guess my customer liked it too. She never actually told me one way or the other, but she didn't return it either. She kept it. And she paid for it. All told, I got six orders for the navy-blue suit. Each one required driving up to Lowell and negotiating another size or a small change to the pattern.

I spent that spring and early summer sending out catalogs and fulfilling catalog orders as they came in. As difficult as the navy-blue suit was to deliver, that was not my only challenge. Not being able to anticipate which items would be the most popular, I ran out of some garments immediately and got stuck with other items. There were two or three pieces that I couldn't even get the manufacturer to deliver, causing me to lose customer orders altogether. This really infuriated me. One of the missing products was a dress from Betty Bailey's showroom. When I called her to see where my order was, she told me that style didn't make the cutting ticket. In other words, the manufacturer didn't get enough orders, so they didn't produce it. Of course she couldn't have cared less that I had a customer order for the dress and that I was going to have to give her money back. The fact that I had a purchase order for that dress style, had photographed it and put it in my catalog made no difference to her either. I was learning about the advantage of controlling your own inventory production. It might have been a pain in the ass to figure out how to make the navy-blue suit, but at least it was within my control.

About five or six weeks after the ads ran, the catalog requests started to trickle down to nothing. And about three weeks after that, the orders dried up too. I had only run my ad one time in the magazine and the newspaper. So naturally the requests didn't go on forever. I guess I viewed the whole process as a test. Spend a finite amount of money and get back a related amount of orders. The idea was to see if I got in more than I spent. I didn't. I counted up my revenue: $3,440. It didn't require accounting genius to figure that the $10,000 I spent to produce the catalog, buy clothes, and advertise was $6,560 more than what I received in orders. That meant a big loss. By this time it was June. I couldn't just rerun my ads now because a lot of my merchandise was spring/summer-related. Short sleeves and light colors and fabrics. It was time to be switching over to fall merchandise. And besides, I didn't have the faith that if I reprinted the catalog and spent more on ads, I would get that money back in revenue. And I'd have to make some changes in the catalog anyway, because some things had sold out. I'd have to either take those things out of the catalog or buy more of them, which I didn't think was possible. Those manufacturers had moved on to the fall season. Of course I still had a big walk-in closet full of maternity clothes. Some people might consider that an asset. I didn't. The whole thing was enough to convince me to hang it up and go get a job.

If I had had more experience in mail order, I might have tried to analyze my catalog requests to see where they were coming from, and what percent converted from requests to orders. I might have evaluated each media advertisement to see whether the *Wall Street Journal* or the *New Yorker* was the more effective. I could have done a better job at studying the merchandise to see what sold, and why. I had naively expected to make a shot in the dark with my little catalog and take down big game. I thought my idea was so brilliant that it would be successful just like that. I didn't realize that businesses take years to perfect and grow. And when I didn't have instant success, I was ready to pack up and go home.

"You give up too easy." Dan was there to prop me up, as usual.

"That's easy for you to say. I just wasted six months. I lost $6,000. I think we can conclude that this business is not successful."

"Don't wimp out now. Look how much you learned. Look at the progress you made. No business ever makes money in the first year. Computer start-ups burn through millions of dollars before they ever make a dime of profit."

"Dan, this isn't a computer business. And we don't *have*

millions of dollars to run through. I mean I could've bought a whole new living room set with the money I spent on my catalog. Something we could get some *use* out of."

"Look, Beck. You have to spend money to make money. It might take you a couple of tries to get it right. But fundamentally nothing has changed. You had a good idea before and it's still a good idea. If you give up now, you'll never know if it could have worked. You have to go try again. Besides, you still have inventory to sell."

That inventory was what got me to try again. I was too cheap to just throw it away. Moreover, I wasn't *quite* ready to say uncle. I was still nursing Isaac, and I didn't want to go back to a real job just then. I figured I'd try one more time. Just one more catalog. I mean, it would be so much easier the second time around. I knew how to get the suit made. I knew how to make and print a catalog. I knew the New York clothing market. Dan was right. I *had* made a lot of progress. True, I had lost $6,560. But I did have all those maternity clothes, which were essentially free to sell in the second catalog. And even though a lot of the styles were specifically spring/summer garments, there were a lot of other styles that were for year-round use. For example, the shirts, the navy-blue suit, and some of the long-sleeved dresses could go into a fall catalog. I could reuse some of the photography, which would save some money, and I also had the knowledge about what had sold and what hadn't. I knew that there was a real market for a maternity suit. And I learned that the $48 basic oxford-cloth shirt in white or blue was an easy pickup for both the career customer and the casual customer who bought it with a pair of jeans. I could have sold more of those shirts, but I ran out of them. I learned that price was enormously important in the whole equation. The one dress I had that was over $175 didn't sell at all, even though I thought it was one of the prettiest ones. In short, I was learning what every buyer knows: how to buy to your customer's taste, not your own. Surely I could do a little better with my second catalog. Couldn't I?

Every setback provides a learning experience if you can get perspective. When you back up and try again, often you see a better way. I have had the good fortune of having had the bad fortune to make me turn around many times in my business life. Staring down the disastrous financial result of my first catalog, I was forced to confront the fundamentals. I *knew* my idea was good. But somehow I just wasn't getting through to my customers. The response to my ads had been tremendous. In fact, I even had to go back and print more copies just to fill all the demand. The problem was those catalog requests didn't convert to merchandise orders. Was the merchandise all wrong? Was it too expensive?

There was only one way to answer those questions. Ask my customers. Or, more accurately, ask my noncustomers, the women who wrote for a catalog and then didn't order from it—my "should have been but weren't" customers. The rest of that week, I stationed myself at my desk and conducted a telephone survey. I went through the return addresses from the catalog requests and tracked down my customers, using directory assistance. Some were home numbers. Some were office numbers. Hospitals. Law offices. Every kind of profession imaginable. Mothers-in-law who were buying presents. And they told me all kinds of things.

"Hi. This is Rebecca Matthias. I'm calling from the Mothers Work Catalog company. Do you have a minute to talk to me?" A little nervous. Not sure what to ask.

"Oh, hi! What a great idea. I wish I'd done that myself. You know I would have ordered a *ton* of stuff but I already bought a lot of awful crappy stuff from a maternity store in the mall. You really should put your catalog out a little earlier in the season." My ads ran in March. I learned that spring apparel catalogs start mailing out in late December, early January. By March, April, it's all over but the crying. Mail-order shoppers buy early in the season.

"I liked the dress on page three but I couldn't quite tell what it looked like in that black-and-white catalog." I learned that apparel catalogs *have* to be in color. Printing it in black and white to save money had to be the worst example of penny-wise and pound-foolishness I came up with. Even though I included the swatch card of fabrics, which my customers liked, it was not a substitute for four-color printing.

"I liked your catalog but I wish you had more in it!" An eight-page catalog? It's hardly worth the postage it takes to mail it. As the saying goes, "You can't sell from an empty cart." If I had actually calculated the total amount of possible revenue from the inventory I owned, I would have realized that even if I had sold every single garment I had bought, my potential revenue would still not have covered the cost of printing, mailing, and advertising the catalog. Even a rudimentary analysis would have achieved better results in my first catalog.

"I was looking for more natural fibers."

"You know, too many of your dresses had short sleeves. I

need long sleeves in my office. With the air-conditioning, it's colder in the summer than in the winter."

"More suits!"

Boy, did I get an ear full. I talked to more than fifty women. I don't think there was a single person who didn't want to talk to me. I was so charged up when I finished, I was convinced I could do better. And I learned—on a gut level—the most important lesson of my business life: to think like a customer. I've said it before, but it wasn't until I conducted my own customer survey, or market analysis as the M.B.A.'s say, that I truly understood that business is all about customers. Their patronage is everything, and understanding their consumer experience is what makes a business succeed. If I had looked at that black-and-white catalog as if I were ordering from it, I would have seen how inadequate it was. Instead, I focused on the cost of creating it. The lost sales from black and white far outweighed the extra expense of color. Even the merchandise selection was lacking in customer orientation. I had simply bought what I could find to fill up the catalog. I *knew* that most of those styles were wrong, but instead of thinking like a customer, I was thinking like a merchant, buying this many dresses, that many blouses, and so forth. Again, if I had just stepped back and looked at the selection like a customer, I would have said, "I would never buy this stuff." So why did I think my customers would?

Now I was consumed with the idea of trying another catalog. But before I could get very far, life intervened. Dan came to an impasse with his business partner and sold his share. We were cast into a sea of financial uncertainty. True, we weren't destitute. We had about $250,000 in the bank, from the sale of Dan's part of his computer business, but we had nothing coming in, and we certainly weren't going to live the rest of our lives on $250,000. All of a sudden our mortgage seemed enormous, and we were reluctant to spend any of our savings on daily living expenses.

It was Sunday morning, and we were brainstorming about our next move. Dan suggested we move in with my parents. I can still picture the Nova and bagels. But suddenly I couldn't take another bite.

"That's a joke, right?" I was very close to my parents, but this seemed a little too close.

"Well . . . not necessarily. I mean we could rent their second-floor apartment and save some money. Besides, I like your parents."

I was skeptical. "I like them too. But that doesn't necessarily mean we should live with them. You're not used to them. They can be really wacky."

The truth was, I was thrilled that Dan brought it up. The idea of having my mother there to help with Isaac was a dream come true. He was ten months old now and he didn't just stay where I put him anymore. It was getting harder and harder to get anything done, and the baby-sitters I was finding were not ideal. They also cost a lot of money and I knew my mother would practically pay me for the opportunity of taking care of Isaac. Both of my parents were semiretired, but still had more energy than I did. It was so tempting to just dump my problems on them. Of course there would be some getting used to each other . . .

I didn't really put up much of a fight. I love Philadelphia. Moving back was in my destiny. My mother had told me so all along. The day the moving van pulled away with all of our belongings, I never looked back. We got in our car and headed south to our new life. We had nothing, and we had everything. No obligations, no baggage, no jobs, no worries. Plenty of nothing. If you've never experienced it, you don't know what you're missing. I was twenty-eight years old, and everything was possible.

How to Buy or Manufacture Your Product

▼ ▼ ▼

How to Buy Product

It's one thing to get an order, it's a whole other story to deliver the product. When I started Mothers Work, my idea was to sell career maternity clothes. My challenge was finding the product and bringing it to the consumer. I ended up buying some clothes and making some.

Most people start out buying their product. After you get a great idea for a business, the next challenge is finding the product. It's out there, but how do you find it and buy it?

Trade shows. Every industry has trade publications and trade shows. You need to find them right away. In 1981 the Internet didn't exist, but if I were starting today, that would be my first stop to locate industry information. Go to the library and look there for trade magazines. Go to the trade shows and talk to everyone who will talk to you. Ask questions. Invest in a business card, which is usually your entrée. No one has to know that your gourmet mustard company is only in the dreaming stages and has never sold a single jar. Fake it when necessary. By the way, this process will tell you volumes about the competitive environment in your industry. Be a sponge and soak up everything they tell you. You may confirm your belief that there is a crying need for your idea, or you may find out that your idea is already being done, which could save you a lot of time, money, and aggravation.

Showrooms. Based on the contacts you make at the trade show, you will want to spend more time at the showrooms of the most promising vendors. Almost every major city has concentrated areas of showrooms for major industries, so you can usually see several related suppliers at once. You can learn a lot by talking to the showroom reps, but you have to ask the right questions. Important questions to ask in a showroom:

▾ *What is your best seller?* You'll be amazed that they'll come right out and tell you. This information is crucial, especially when you're just starting out and have no sales history to go on. If I had asked the sales reps this question when I bought clothes for my first catalog, I would have learned some very basic things. For example, white shirts will sell almost twice as much as the next-best-selling color, so you need to buy proportionately.

▾ *Whom do you sell to / who is your biggest customer?* There's nothing like knowing your enemy. If you can find out who the competition is and what they'll be carrying next season, maybe you can do something about it. For example, if you're competing on price, you might want to put in a big order for the same item and discount it.

▾ *What is the suggested retail price?* In some cases, usually larger, more established vendors, retail price is strongly suggested. The merchandise may even arrive preticketed at that price. Although it is illegal for vendors to price-fix by dictating the retail price, they can *suggest* it. And you may find that if you discount their products without their permission, it may be difficult to get them to fill your future orders. Of course the market usually prevents pricing above the competition because consumers are too smart to pay more at your store than somewhere else. Even the smaller vendors will tell you at what price their other accounts are typically retailing their products, so you can get some idea of what your markup will be.

▾ *What are your minimums?* When you are just starting out, your orders will be small compared to other accounts. Some of the bigger manufacturers set minimum order quantities that could preclude your order altogether. Obviously you need to determine this before going too far.

▾ *Do you give volume discounts?* They won't advertise it, but you can usually negotiate a discount for a big order. The question is how big is big? It depends on the vendor and how meaningful your order is to him. It never hurts to ask.

▾ *What are your credit terms?* Always try to get as much credit as possible. Every industry has different practices on credit. For example, in fabric companies usually your invoice is payable sixty days after delivery. You can expect a 2 percent discount if you pay early—on or just before delivery. In the apparel business many vendors use what is called an "8 in 10, EOM" policy, which means you can take an 8 percent discount if you pay on or before the tenth of the month in the month following receipt of the order. This ridiculously complicated policy grew from retailers' inventory planning method of rushing everything into the store by the end of the month for sales expected to be made in the following month. Vendors were rewarded for being on time with their deliveries by being paid by the tenth of the following month if they met the end-of-month deadline.

▾ *What is the lead time on my order? How about on reorders?* You should place a premium on quick deliveries. If you have to order way in the future, you won't get the responsiveness you need for a growing business. Reorders are crucial. If you find out that your sales take off in a certain item and you can't get back into it, then you'll lose sales, because you'll run out of product. Quick response is even more important than lowest cost, because sales are the lifeblood of a growth company.

▾ *Will you put my label on your products?* Usually a larger order is required to get the vendor to put your label on a product. Obviously this is a great way to promote your own brand if they'll do it. Sometimes the vendor will *add* your label to their own. It's probably a long shot for a start-up small company, but I'd put the whole question in the "it doesn't hurt to ask" category.

Placing the Order and Taking Delivery of the Product

Ordering. Place your orders in writing on a purchase order. A purchase order can be as simple as a form you make on your PC, or you can buy a generic form from the office supply store. Every purchase order must have a "start ship" date and a cancel date. Don't let your vendor ship at his convenience. Get an agreement on a window of delivery time. Also be sure to include the agreed-upon payment terms and the ship-to address. Often the billing address is different from the ship-to address.

Shipping and delivery. You will pay for the shipment of the product, so if you have a preference, be sure to specify the shipping method on your purchase order. For some products, especially big-ticket items like furniture, instead of buying the inventory and holding it, you may be able to get the supplier to drop-ship directly to your customer. This can really help the cash flow because you don't have to buy inventory ahead and hold it until you get an order.

Discounts. Never pay full price for merchandise that arrives late, damaged, or not exactly as it was ordered. Negotiate a discount. Even if you think you can get full price for the merchandise, take advantage of the vendor's mistake and use it to make money! After all, you had an agreement to pay a certain amount of money for a certain product, and if the vendor doesn't deliver, you shouldn't pay.

Customer returns. If you get returns from your customer due to manufacturers' flaws, you need to push the product back to the manufacturer for a credit. Sometimes, defects don't show up until they're used or washed. Usually you can't just ship them back to the vendor. You need to get an agreement from the vendor to take them back, in the form of a return goods authorization (RGA). Hopefully you will have an unpaid bill or a future order to deduct the credit from. Otherwise it will be very hard to collect a refund.

Co-op advertising. Retailers have always leveraged their advertising budgets by doing co-op ads with manufacturers. After all, your vendor will be benefiting just as much as you by the advertisement of his product, so why not split the cost?

How to Make Product

Okay, I'll grant you that this topic is rather big to be covered in a few paragraphs. Let me just give you a little food for thought. If your idea involves manufacturing a new product, then you have a big challenge ahead of you. But you also have a product that no one else has.

Patents and trademarks. If you really invent something new and proprietary, you must invest the money to see a lawyer about patenting it or protecting it in some way. My maternity suit was not "patentable," but I did have a few ideas further down the road that were, including a specially constructed expandable waistband. Your lawyer will help you determine whether your product is distinctive and different enough to be patented. You should also think about trademarking your company name or the name of your store or catalog. This will involve a name search by your attorney to find all the registered company names to be sure it's not already in use, and then registering the name. You don't want to invest a lot of marketing and advertising in your company name only to receive a certified letter a few years later from an attorney telling you to cease and desist from using your company name because someone else claimed it first. This actually happened to me in the case of Mimi Maternity, a fashion maternity division I started in 1990 which I named after my sister Mimi. Sometime later I was informed that the name was already being used in Miami in a three-store chain of maternity stores. Ultimately I had to buy the name from that owner, paying $30,000.

Design. Depending on what your new product is, you may need the help of designers and contractors. Freelance is the way to go here because you certainly don't want to be hiring people while you're starting up. For the first three or four years I used freelance patternmakers. They would work from either a sketch or a sample garment and produce a pattern for somewhere between $50 and $150 per pattern, depending on the complexity of the style and the number of pattern pieces. Local schools are good ways to hook up with freelancers. You can also take out a classified ad in the right trade journal, or, as always, try the yellow pages. The fact that other people design and make your product does not take away the ownership of the idea from you. As long as you own the idea, the patent, the trademark, the distribution of the product, then you own the *brand.* And the brand is the asset. For example, Rachel's Brownies can be made by subcontractor cooking shops, or various moms working at home, or anywhere else. Rachel could even hire a master chef to come up with a great recipe for her brownies. But if they are packaged in the trademarked Rachel's Brownies packaging, in the familiar logo that Rachel's Brownies uses and that has been advertised on the radio and on billboards, then Rachel is the owner of the brand, regardless of who actually designed and made the product.

Production. Many new products are produced as a cottage industry when the volumes are small, and then a more professional contractor handles larger volumes later on. Cottage industry just means a small-scale unorganized or unprofessional network of producers, often home-based. For example, many handmade apparel products, like hand-knit sweaters or silk-screen printed knit tops, start out in that way. However you start out, the important thing in setting up your manufacturing is to make it "quick response." Don't accept long lead times and slow production.

Customer feedback. In order to be customer-driven, you have to listen to customer demand and then be right there with the product. That means measuring the sales of every item immediately when they happen, and then having the right color, the right size, the right item based on what is selling. If you buy all your inventory way ahead of getting sales information, you may have the wrong assortment. You need to devise a way of doing business that is "make it as you go" and allows for customer input, flexibility, and speed to market.

A business is all about selling a product to a customer. Whether that product is a commodity, a unique item, or a service, it is the basis of your success. And whether you buy it or make it, be sure it is a reflection of your customers' desires.

Chapter Three Checklist

▾ Most business owners start out buying their product. Use trade shows and showrooms to look for it.

▾ In determining what to buy, ask wholesalers what their bestsellers are in your category.

▾ Ask your wholesalers who their best customer is to learn who your competitors are and what their offerings will be.

▾ Ask wholesalers if there is a minimum order size, whether or not they give volume discounts, what the credit terms are, and what lead time there is in initial orders and reorders.

▾ Ask about shipping and delivery, co-op advertising, and return policies for defective products.

▾ If you create your own products, you must patent or brand them in some way.

▾ Don't accept long lead times and slow production.

▾ Always gather customer feedback to make sure what you are selling reflects customers' desires.

chapter four

Asking for Help

The next year of my life was probably one of the most exciting ever. So much happened. Things I never dreamed possible. Later when I went through doors that closed behind me, I ran into walls. I learned that I wasn't invincible. But all that came later. For now I was on top of the world and nothing could stop me.

We moved into the second-floor apartment of my parents' town house in downtown Philadelphia. I grew up in this house and now I was returning. My parents, Leon and Wilma, live in an area called Society Hill, which is the historic section of Philadelphia, where the houses have historic plaques saying that William Penn slept here or Benjamin Franklin invented the printing press here. Being surrounded by the memories of so many trailblazing entrepreneurial Americans gave me a charge. We put most of our furniture in storage, keeping just enough to furnish the little two-bedroom apartment. It seemed like an adventure.

We settled into a routine: me working on my catalog and Dan writing his book. My mother was working part-time as a nurse at Pennsylvania Hospital, but she still managed to spend more time taking care of Isaac than I did. As soon as she got home at three in the afternoon, Isaac would end up downstairs with her so I could get something done. Every night we would eat at my parents'. We cooked dinner on a rotation system, each of us taking one night, including my father and Dan, and then one night each week we'd eat out at a different funky restaurant in the city. Never anything expensive but always exotic. It was sort of like living in a commune. None of us had a nine-to-five job. We were all on a flextime schedule before the term was dreamed up. And all of us shared responsibility for Isaac. My father used to wheel him around the city wherever he went. All of the ladies in the neighborhood knew him and looked for him in the little playgrounds and parks: a gray-haired man pushing an adorable baby in a cheap fold-up stroller at all hours of the day and night.

Dan was thrilled to be starting something new. He loved doing things he had never done before, and it was a huge relief to be out of the computer business. His novel was going well. He would get up around 4:45 A.M. and get right to work on it. He has always been a morning person and now he could make his own schedule. By the time I got up at seven he'd be well into it. After breakfast I'd be trying to get my second catalog going, and he'd be running out of steam. By around ten he'd stall out and wander over to my desk.

"I've been thinking about your brand awareness. I think you need to have your own label in your clothes. That way your customers will be reminded of Mothers Work every time they put their clothes on and see the label. It's like free advertising."

I resisted. "They're not my clothes. I mean, I didn't manufacture them. What do you think I'm going to do, rip out the label and sew mine in?"

"That would work." He was nodding.

"Dan, that's ridiculous. I could get *sued.* Besides, I don't have time to be ripping out labels on every order I get."

"Well then, just leave the old label in and put a Mothers Work label in too. You know, sort of like 'Armani, for Mothers Work.' Saks would do that. You've got to start thinking about your *brand.*" Dan loved marketing. And thinking about marketing for Mothers Work was a perfect way to procrastinate about writing his novel. "How long could it take to sew on a label? Two minutes? Do you think it's worth two minutes to increase your brand awareness?"

Every morning he'd dream up another way to improve my mail-order business. His ideas were usually terrific, but they all involved me doing one more thing that I didn't have time for. After all, he had the luxury of thinking globally. I was trying to actually print this catalog. I didn't have a staff or even an assistant, and I was already stretched so thin I couldn't do one more thing. One morning he stretched me to the breaking point.

"You know, I think you'd get more bang out of your advertising if you had more information about what publications your customers read. Why don't you try to organize a focus group and get more information before you place your ads this time?"

It was a reasonable suggestion, but there was no way on this earth that I could make time for all that. "I don't have time to do that. I have to place all my ads by Friday or I'll miss the deadlines."

"How much time could it take? You could be wasting all your money on all the wrong—"

"Dan, I have six million things to do this week, and it's my turn to cook tomorrow, and I haven't opened a new post-office box yet, which has to go into the ad copy for replies, and I still haven't finished buying the new dresses I want to get from Betty Bailey to put into the catalog, and I *don't have time to do a focus group!"* I was getting all worked up and screaming. Isaac looked up from where he was crawling around and started to cry.

Dan picked Isaac up and thought that over. "You know, you get this negative attitude sometimes, and you miss opportunities."

"Look, I think the focus group is a great idea. But there are only twenty-four hours in a day. I need help!"

There I said it. That statement landed like a big package in the middle of the room waiting to be opened. At first neither one of us wanted to touch it. I need help. I need your help. Join my business and it will be *ours,* not *mine.* We weren't opposed to working together. After all, we had discussed the possibility from the very beginning of our marriage. And I had worked in Dan's business. Why couldn't he get behind something I had started? On the other hand, did we really want to start down this road?

"Well, I guess I could work on your marketing a little. I could give it a few hours a day when I'm tired of writing."

Of course it wasn't long before a few hours became a partnership. And we have been working side by side ever since. As with other major life-changing decisions I've made, it seems like I slid into it. But sometimes what may seem like serendipity is actually the culmination of a series of events that come together in an instant. In some ways Dan and I had been moving toward that moment our whole lives, and it shaped our future together.

The second catalog hit in early September of 1982. I had taken many of the customer comments of my telephone survey and used them to improve my catalog. I included some new selections, including a suit in several colors, and I used a combination of color photography and black and white. I increased my advertising budget and Dan organized a publicity campaign to try to get the attention of magazines and newspapers to do editorial coverage. We were really moving in high gear, and I was exhausted all the time. I finally realized it wasn't just all the hard work. I was pregnant again.

"This is going to be great for editorial interest." Always the marketer, Dan was ready to get some benefit out of our new state. "Pregnant woman starts business for other pregnant yuppie women who have delayed pregnancy to pursue careers and now need career maternity clothes. Throw in entrepreneurial mail-order element and demographic trends, and every editor will find something appealing to write about. You can model your own maternity clothes in the picture."

In fact, that was not far from what happened. We sent out press releases with the catalog to every publication we could think of. Business editors, fashion editors, general interest editors. Everything from *Good Housekeeping* to *Crain's New York Business*. The press release was just a one-page description of the business which had some statistics about the new trend of career women in their thirties having babies. It had some personal information about me and all my degrees and showed how I personified the whole demographic trend. It really was a whole article in itself, written so that if an editor needed a fill-in story for either the lifestyle section or the business section of a magazine or newspaper, she could just lift the whole press release and use it.

We went to the newsstand and bought all the magazines we thought might be interested in the story and looked up the lifestyle, beauty, and business editors' names listed in the front of the publication and sent them off. Back then the whole topic of women having careers and babies together was hot, and our story was a natural for publication. And *they actually wrote stories about Mothers Work.* About us! *Working Woman* magazine did a story. The *Philadelphia Inquirer* did a feature story on the front of the lifestyle section. At one point, one of the wire services picked up the press release and put it in their news summary, and lots of little papers in small towns used it as filler. My customers would clip the article out and send it along with $2 for a catalog, so I would see all the little papers no one ever hears of that carried the story.

The editors and reporters would call me sometimes for my comments and quotes. Dan would always try to answer the phone in case it was a reporter, so it didn't sound like I was the only person in the office. ("I'll see if she's available.") I would try like crazy to get the post-office box address into the story so that people could order the catalog. At the very least I'd try to get them to say "Philadelphia-based company," so my customers could reach us through directory assistance.

When the *Wall Street Journal* wanted to do a story, I nearly fell on the floor. I loved the *Wall Street Journal.* It was my yuppie business bible. They wanted to talk to a few of my customers, so I gave them my older sister Ruth's number. She and I were both pregnant, due a week apart, and I knew I could count on her to say the right thing. She is an obstetrician, and she was practicing in Washington, D.C., at the time. I thought the "baby" theme of her profession was perfect. I never actually told the *Wall Street Journal* that she was my sister. I mean, why should I? She was a Harvard Medical School–trained doctor in her thirties having her first baby, so she fit the profile exactly. I told her to sound like an executive and tell them she wore suits all the time when she was in the hospital. Miraculously the article ran on the second-section front page with all kinds of quotes from Dr. Ruth Crane about how she couldn't have lived as a pregnant obstetrician without Mothers Work clothes. The customer response from that article was unbelievably strong. I must have had two hundred catalog requests from really quality customers.

My business was booming from all the publicity we were getting. And I was walking about three feet off the ground with the recognition. I felt like I was really going somewhere. The peak media experience was when the *Good Morning America* show called and said they were interested in doing a five-minute piece on Mothers Work for their business section. They sent an entire camera crew down from New York to follow me around for a day, and they ended with a clip of us eating spaghetti at my parents' house.

We were working crazy hours trying to keep up with everything, and I was getting bigger and bigger. Since we had no employees yet, we were doing everything. Every day we had to keep up with taking orders over the phone and by mail, then packing them up in boxes and shipping them out by UPS. We were probably getting between fifteen and twenty orders a day. At the same time I would be designing new styles for the next catalog, and also going on buying trips to New York. The new styles would involve finding a patternmaker, buying fabric, buttons, and other trims, and then negotiating the cut and sew work with the three or four sewing contractors we had located. Then, of course, I had to keep up with all of the accounting work, bill paying, inventory management, and other paperwork.

Isaac was one year old and required more of our attention. Even the weekly dinners that Dan and I were responsible for were becoming impossible to manage. It was clear that we needed some help. For the first time since we'd had Isaac, we finally faced the fact that we needed some serious child care. We were facing what so many families face today, especially mothers who want or need to work. No two mothers find the same solution to child care, but many mothers are saddled with the burden of guilt if and when they leave their child under someone else's supervision. In my now vast experience hiring domestic assistants, I have prioritized the importance of certain qualities they possess, and trusted that with these qualities nothing could go too terribly wrong. Number one is kindness toward my children. Number two is trustworthiness and reliability. Keeping up with the laundry is somewhere in the middle. Cooking and cleaning are way down on the list. It took me a few tries before I found the right person and got my priorities straight.

My mother found a classified ad in the local paper for "Woman looking for part-time housework/child care. Can cook." I called her, and when she showed up right on time the next day, looking like someone's sweet grandmother, I took it as a good sign. Isaac was wrapped around my legs, staring at her, holding on for dear life.

"Where do you keep the TV, dear?" she asked after a cursory walk around the apartment. She seemed incredulous when I told her we didn't have one. I wanted to go into all the alternative ways to pass the time besides TV, including taking Isaac to the park, reading him a book, playing with Legos, having him trail around while *cleaning* the apartment, but I was late for a meeting with a new sewing contractor. So I simply took a minute to ask her to make something—anything—for dinner and told her I'd definitely be back by five. It would just be a few hours, I told myself. And she looked so *nice.* I know you're not supposed to sneak out when your child is not looking because it destroys the trusting bond you have built, but I was really late, and I *had* to.

I remember worrying about Isaac all day. I knew my mother would be home by three. Surely he would be okay until then. It's not that Dan didn't care about Isaac or that he shirked his obligation to share the housework and child care, it was just that it wasn't gut-wrenching for him to leave Isaac the way it was for me. He didn't struggle with his identity as a parent when forced to hire a baby-sitter the way I did. Likewise, if we hadn't been able to find someone to help with the housework and dinner, and we had to eat at McDonald's every night, Dan would have chalked it up as a necessary side effect of starting up a business, whereas I would have felt like a pathetic excuse for a mother. Of course mixed in with my worrying was the exhilaration of finally being able to get something done. I had an entire afternoon child-free and I whirled around from one thing to the next.

When I walked into the apartment at 5:01, my baby-sitter was sitting on the windowsill with her coat on. She stood up and walked by me. "Supper's on the stove. The baby's with your mother downstairs. I quit."

As she walked by me I heard her muttering to herself "no TV." I called my mother to make sure Isaac was okay. Then I went into the kitchen and looked at the mess she called supper, which was simmering in a pan on top of the stove. Dan had come in two minutes behind me as our baby-sitter was leaving. He got the drift. We both stared at our supper for a minute, and then we looked at each other and started to laugh. Pretty soon we were uncontrollably hysterical. Back to Friendly's, our home away from home.

The next sitter I hired turned out better. She genuinely loved taking care of Isaac, but she couldn't really handle much else. Reliability was maybe 6 on a scale of 1 to 10, but luckily I had my extended family to help on those days when she was late or didn't show up. And besides, I was working at home, so it wasn't a major crisis.

I took advantage of my new (relative) freedom to go to an all-day conference in New York for women starting businesses. I took the train up and went to the Sheraton Hotel, a monstrously huge building, filled that day with professional-looking women, all streaming into the mezzanine level where the conference was being held. They were carrying their briefcases, wearing suits, and looking very serious. There must have been five hundred women in attendance. I felt happy to be a part of the group. I guess I hadn't realized how lonely and isolating my mail-order business was. Dan was just as happy keeping his own company, but I needed social interaction and professional peers to validate my activities. I spent the day going to various seminars on subjects like "How to Account for Your Profits" and "Dealing with Growth."

The keynote speaker at lunch was Debbie Fields, the founder of Mrs. Fields Cookies. Her company had $160 million in revenue, and she had started it from nothing, selling cookies from a little hole in a wall in a strip mall in California. She said when business was slow, she would put little cookie samples on a tray and run out in the parking lot giving them away to anyone she ran into. She was so animated about her business and her chocolate chip cookies that she made your mouth water just listening to her. She had three young daughters that she took everywhere with her, and her husband worked with her, developing an amazing computer system to support the hundreds of stores she now had all over the country. After she spoke she breezed off the stage and headed to her private jet, which would whisk her back to Utah, where she lived a glamorous life next to a ski resort. She was my hero. I hung on every word she said and decided right there and then that I was going to be like her. If she could do it, why on this earth couldn't I? I rode home on the train dreaming about my future life.

The next few weeks I was a woman on a mission. I was creating a mail-order empire. Every box I addressed was a building block in my castle of dreams. I would race around during the day, sending packages, working on future catalogs, keeping track of bills and receipts, and working on publicity. Every night after dinner we would address catalogs from the day's telephone and mail requests. My mother would type the names and addresses into our little PC, which had a primitive mail-order software package. Dan and I would stuff and lick.

And my father would take Isaac for a stroll. The occasional dinner guest would be drafted into service.

Meanwhile I was approaching labor and delivery for my second baby. My sister Ruth and I had practically the same due date. But mine came and went and still I didn't go into labor. Ruth went first. Since it was her first baby, my mother felt she had to go to Washington to help her. I had mixed feelings about letting her go. I knew I was hogging all of her attention, but I *needed* her more. My sister's life was meticulous compared to mine. She practically had her kitchen alphabetically organized, for Christ sake. I barely managed to find the salt shaker. My mother would only get in Ruth's way.

"We'll only be gone for a week," she said as she was getting the last few things into her suitcase. She wasn't even leaving my father to help me. I was in her house, on the first floor, sort of moping around. My baby-sitter was cleaning up in our apartment, making a big show of vacuuming, hauling my mother's vacuum cleaner up the stairs, since I didn't even have one. I had a sense of foreboding, but I was trying to be grown-up. Suddenly we heard a loud series of bumps and screams cascading down the stairway. We both ran out to the hall and found my babysitter moaning at the bottom of the steps with the vacuum cleaner all wrapped around her. This was my helper while my mother was gone. She meant well but she never quite pulled it together. We got her all unraveled and sent her home for the rest of the day.

About two days after my parents left I went into labor in the middle of the night. We left Isaac with the neighbors and walked the three blocks to the hospital, and I barely got undressed before Josh was born with one long push. Dan practically had to catch him, because the doctor was still scrubbing up. Josh started out with an easy approach to life, which he still has. He did, however, throw the rest of our lives into chaos. When I went home two days later, my mother was not there to hand the baby to. There was no pot roast in the oven. Dan was not relaxed and sipping something on the couch. He was running around like a crazy person trying to keep the business going, and taking care of Isaac too. The sink was piled high with dirty dishes, but I was in no condition to do anything about it. My back, which had always been defective, had simply collapsed the day Josh was born. I have a condition called scoliosis, which is a degenerative side-to-side curving of the spine. I had been able to live with the occasional back pain most of my life, but now I could hardly get out of bed in the morning. When we walked into the house, I made it as far as my parents' bedroom on the first floor. The stairs up to our apartment were simply out of the question, so Josh and I lived in their bedroom till my parents got home.

On my second day home Ruth and my mother called to see how I was doing. Ruth, of course, was totally recovered, and they were doing things like going to the movies and out to dinner. I tried valiantly to keep a brave face, but it was clear what a mess things were.

"Do you want me to come home?" my mother asked. Oh sure, then I would be responsible for depriving Ruth of "first baby" help.

"Nooo," I sniveled. "You don't have to. I'm okay."

My mother hung up the phone and started to pack.

When my parents got home, things improved vastly, but my physical condition was clearly not going to rebound. Isaac was one and a half years old now, and the combination of two in diapers, plus a business "in diapers," plus a back in shambles was challenging to say the least. When I finally went to an orthopedic surgeon, he didn't mince words. He told me that my back was never going to get any better, and it would probably get a lot worse, and if I didn't have major back surgery where he cut my entire back open and straightened it and then fused every vertebra except one together, and stuck a metal rod in there for good measure, then I would probably die young, in a slow and agonizing way. And there was a .8 percent chance that I would die in the operating room and a .5 percent chance that I would be paralyzed for life.

Once I reconciled all that in my mind and realized that surgery was inevitable, I wanted to get it done as quickly as possible. Between surgery and recovery, I was going to be pretty much out of it for two or three months. It's times like these when you better hope you picked the right partner in life. I can't say it was easy, but somehow Dan pulled me through the whole ugly ordeal. Having moved home at this point in time was not a bad thing either. My mother pretty much took over as substitute mother for Isaac and Josh, and my father agreed to fill in for me at Mothers Work. He kept the bills organized and also took over most of the sewing subcontractor work.

The year was 1984 and my business was starting to plateau. I had just taken a major ride at exhilarating speed, and now things had slowed down to a crawl and I was about to not only slow way down but actually take a few big steps backward. I can tell you from my experience that a business start-up is not always full speed ahead in a forward direction. My resolve was about to be tested.

The Ten Commandments of Combining a New Business with a New Family

▼ ▼ ▼

I'll be honest: this part is really more useful for women than men. I think men have a long tradition of combining work and family, and if anything, they have learned some of these commandments to a fault. Besides, women are "hormonally challenged" when it comes to issues concerning their children. Guilt and peer pressure get thrown into the mix to color their perceptions as well.

It was helpful to me to have role models in women who successfully combined being a mom and running a business. Verna Gibson, who has been a member of my board of directors for many years, was always an inspiration to me. When she joined The Limited as a buyer, in 1971, it was a chain of eight stores selling contemporary clothes with a combined annual revenue of $4 million. She had two daughters, aged seven and eight. While raising them, she climbed up the corporate ladder, first as vice-president, then executive vice-president, and finally president of The Limited, which she went on to grow into a $1.5-billion-revenue company. Recently I asked her if she thought being a mother affected her business life. She told me that she learned patience and understanding as a mother, which helped her in managing people in her business. Although she, too, admitted that maternal guilt intruded into her life at times, she said in regards to raising her children, "At the end of the day we did a pretty good job." Her two daughters, now grown with families of their own, have collaborated in a new store that sells Amish-made furniture. Verna says her daughters thank her for giving them exposure into the business world and the confidence to start their own business. Compared to their friends, they said, "those people didn't have the direction we had." I've met Verna's daughters and they are generous and well-rounded women who obviously adore their mother. I would have to conclude that Verna had two successes in her life—business and family—and that her life has been richer for it.

Although the Ten Commandments of Combining a New Business with a New Family may be more helpful to women, I hope that any men in the audience will stay with me, because at the very least you will gain some insight into your significant other's tortured mind. And remember, your children are 50 percent your responsibility too. So how do you all of a sudden accomplish twice as much as you used to? And stay sane.

1. Remember that you're doing this because you want to. No one is putting a gun to your head to start this business and to have kids at the same time. It so happens that the optimum time in your life to do both occurs right around the twenty-five-to-thirty-five age, so many of us end up in this crazy situation. But let's get rid of that martyr syndrome right at the outset. You're doing this because you want to achieve greatness. Because you have a burning desire to rule your destiny. Because you need the rush that comes with creating something out of sheer nothingness. And let's face it: you *really want to make a lot of money.* No one is going to hand it to you. Any of it. You're going to work your ass off for it. And you're going to sacrifice. You could have stuck with your reliable paycheck or devoted yourself entirely to the kids, but instead you're going to be racing around trying to get the order, or the bank loan, or the next day's payroll. Because you're in it for the long haul. Your rewards will come later. And they'll be bigger than you dreamed possible. Please don't misunderstand me. I'm not saying your children aren't important. They are the *most important* thing there is in life. But life is not a zero-sum game. The fact that you do other things in life doesn't *take away* from what you do with your children. It's up to you to decide what you want out of life. Make a choice and then make it happen. Do it for yourself. And as hard as things get, never give up. Remember, you're doing this because you want to.

2. You are not superman/superwoman. Don't try to do more than is humanly possible here on earth. There are only twenty-four hours in the day. And there is only so much you can accomplish in that time. Start prioritizing your life and get rid of all the extraneous activities that you can live without, at least for the next few years. Like Saturday night movies (forget it—you're going to be polishing up your business plan); dinner parties (unless your business is a Martha Stewart knockoff); bake-sale committees for your children's nursery school; charity events; hobbies; lunch with friends—you get the idea. Give up to get more. Focus your life on the few things you really care about. Your new business and your children, certainly. *Maybe* one more thing. I'm not saying you can never go back to teaching Sunday school or volunteering at the local Girl Scout troop. And I'm certainly not saying these aren't worthwhile activities. I'm simply saying that if you overextend yourself, your business will not be as successful as it could be, and you'll be worn-out and not very happy. Just accept the fact that you're not superman/superwoman and that you've made a choice in your life for right now, and move on with it.

3. Do not deal in guilt. In my experience most mothers feel guilty—whether they work outside the home or inside the home. If you can free yourself from this useless and harmful emotion, your life will be happier and more productive. And your children's lives will be too. Your son can forgive you for missing an event or postponing his birthday party because of an important event in *your* life. The key is to be honest and open about your actions. Say what you can do and what you can't do and then be sure to live up to it. Share your hopes and dreams with your children so they will know why you are working so hard, and can share in your achievements, and so they'll have some appreciation for why you can't always be at every event. Then cut yourself a break and don't give in to the guilts. You will be training your children to live their own independent lives. When it comes time for them to have their own activities without involving you, they won't feel guilty either. You may not be able to go to every school function, but remember that you are giving them something very valuable—a role model of someone who has a dream and is working hard to get it. Your children will be very proud of you.

4. Get help. You may not be able to afford a full-time housekeeper, cook, or nanny. But believe me you can't do it all yourself. You have much bigger fish to fry, and help is not a luxury, it is a requirement. Repeat: help is a requirement. I have seen too many women who feel guilty about getting help in maintaining their house because they feel it's their moral obligation to vacuum, clean the bathroom, and do all the child care even when they are starting a business or running a business or working outside the home. They have never learned to value their time and they don't realize that when they take an hour or two to make dinner instead of sending out for a hamburger, they are taking time away from much more valuable things they could have been doing to advance their business. They find it much easier to do it themselves than get the help they need. And the sad consequence is that either they drive themselves crazy or they never get their business off the ground or both! You may have to get creative if you're short on funds, and, as I did, you may have to put up with second-rate help, but it's better than taking precious time from your business and doing it yourself. High school students don't cost much and they're energetic. If you have a reasonable relationship with your mother, don't be proud—call on her. Invite your elderly aunt to move in with you in exchange for making dinner. Somehow, some way, get the help you need to focus on your business.

5. Leverage your time. With the very little time you have, you have to make it work double time. Don't do fluff stuff. You don't have time for that anymore. For example, *never* bake cookies for the class bake sale. Your child couldn't care less if you bake brownies, or if you buy Sara Lee or Ring Dings (he or she would probably prefer Ring Dings). The bake-off is a worthy but luxurious activity for mothers who have more time than you do. This is what I call fluff stuff. If you want to make a difference to your child, once or twice a year carve out an hour to go to school and talk to the class, sharing a hobby (that you used to have) or talking about your business (my kids always loved it when I did this). This doesn't take a lot of time, and it is a meaningful hour to the person that matters. Your child. Not the teacher, not the other parents, not you. Don't spend your small amount of time on parent committees or teacher projects. It takes much more time than you can afford right now. If you should ever find yourself with an extra hour at the end of the day, go somewhere with the kids. Do *not* bake a pie and make lasagna from scratch. As a matter of fact, the less you make dinner the better. Go to McDonald's. Heat something up in the microwave. Eat at your mother's house. Making dinner is one of the biggest time wasters that women face. Your time is your most valuable commodity right now. Don't give it away. Figure out which jobs or chores absolutely need your input and only do those things. For example, buying clothes for the kids was one thing I never assigned because I wanted to have some control over my children's appearance and train them in taking care of themselves. So twice a year, at the beginning of each season, I would take all three of them to the mall and buy hundreds of dollars of clothes for the entire season. It's much better to do bulk buying than to constantly be out of hats and gloves or to come up short when your daughter needs a dress for the holiday program, and it leverages a few hours of your time. Helping the kids with homework was another job that I felt needed my or Dan's input. So we put aside an hour every night to do just that. The key is to identify important jobs and have a definite time for them, so they always get done but don't invade every corner of your day. Then delegate everything else to the baby-sitter or whomever you have to help you.

6. Organize your life, and your business will follow. If you're not an organized person, get that way. Fast. Forget about that freewheeling, spontaneous person you used to be. You're in the army now. You will have more time with the kids if you have an organized routine that builds that time in. For example, at our house dinner as a family at 6:00 sharp has always been sacrosanct. Unless Dan and I are out of town, we all sit down together. Breakfast is the same. It takes some organization to make that happen, but once you set it up, it's like breathing in and out every day. Everyone knows what is expected and there are very, very few exceptions. Now, you may not be able to accomplish this particular routine. Maybe your husband isn't your business partner, and maybe he works second shift. Or maybe your business involves being out of the house at dinnertime. You need to develop your own schedule.

If you don't build a weekly routine in an organized and predictable way, you won't be able to round up the troops on a whim. Other household chores and obligations as well as pleasures should be handled with the same amount of organization. Take your child to nursery school every Tuesday and spend time with his/her teacher. Read the paper between 6:00 and 6:20 A.M. Get on a schedule, and you will accomplish more.

7. Take care of your marriage. Did I forget to say that your spouse or partner is one of the highest (maybe *the* highest) priorities in your life? If he/she is not behind this project, then I advise you to drop it right now. Whether or not your spouse is involved in your business, he will still be critical to its success. You will need to support each other throughout this process, and it won't be easy. Don't neglect your partner. Yes, this means making time for him or her, but more important, it means making him or her your spiritual partner. The one you share all your thoughts, problems, achievements, hopes, and disappointments with. Don't shut him out. You're going to be on a big roller-coaster ride of highs and lows, and you're going to need him for lots and lots of emotional support. And if you expect him to be there for you, you'd better make sure you do the same.

8. Lower your housekeeping standards. I was lucky here. It never bothered me too much when spiderwebs accumulated in every corner of the apartment. Or when mold grew in the pot that had been left on the back burner of the stove for a week. I was never a housecleaning fanatic. So I was able to focus on my business without being overly distracted by the need to clean house. If you find yourself sweeping the stairs at 11:00 P.M. because you can't stand a little dust, then grab yourself and shake hard. It's not that important! You have much more important things to worry about. You're building an empire. Do you think Steve Jobs ever cleaned out his garage when he was inventing the personal computer? No! He didn't have time for insignificant crap like that. And you don't either. If your mother-in-law doesn't like it, then good, she can cook Thanksgiving dinner at her house next year, where it's clean.

9. Be kind to yourself. This can mean the occasional manicure or night at the movies *(very* occasional). But what I really mean is don't be too hard on yourself when you miss the class play and all the other mothers were there. Or when your business isn't rocketing to success and you start to doubt your abilities. Or when your house is a mess. You have the guts to try what others only talk about and wish they did their whole lives. You are challenging yourself right to the limit. Don't beat yourself up when you fall short of your own expectations. Give yourself a big pep talk and send yourself back out to try again. Be your biggest supporter. If you don't believe in yourself, then it's for sure no one else will.

10. Life is short. Enjoy yourself.

Chapter Four Checklist

▼ Remember, you're doing this because you want to.

▼ Don't try to do more than is humanly possible. Prioritize your life and get rid of extraneous activities.

▼ Don't feel guilty because of a missed event. Cut yourself a break.

▼ Get help. You cannot do everything yourself.

▼ Leverage your time. Do those things only *you* can do and delegate everything else.

▼ Organize your life. You'll have more time for your business and your family if you have a routine or schedule.

▼ Take care of your marriage. You can only succeed if your partner is behind you. Don't shut him or her out.

▼ Lower your housekeeping standards. You have more important things to worry about.

▼ Be kind to yourself. You should be your biggest supporter.

▼ Life is short. Enjoy.

chapter five

The Toddler Years

My Company Learns to Walk

I've said it before, but I'd like to reemphasize it here in case there are any doubts left: my business was not an overnight success. It has been more like the Sisyphus experience, doomed to pushing the rock up the hill forever, than the Icarus experience, soaring to the sun. The time after my surgery stays in my mind as the lowest of the low. The initial days of growing the business and doing everything in an exhilarating trial-by-fire fashion had turned into the endless days of drudgery. Sales had plateaued at a level just short of showing anything like a profit, let alone paying out an actual salary. The business was almost three years old and we were still living above my parents' house, although we had moved into the third-floor apartment and situated the business in the second-floor apartment. My inventory hung from the ceiling in the office, and we worked below the rows of garments. We had been talking for months about renovating and expanding our third-floor apartment into the attic, but we didn't have the money to do it.

In a ridiculous fit of frustration Dan had decided to do his own renovation. After dinner he picked up a Heavy Hammer and started knocking down the walls. At the time, we all applauded, but very soon, lacking time, money, and a meaningful set of architectural plans, our little project came to a standstill. Our daily life resembled the nightly news with its images of wartime Beirut. There were holes in the floorboard, and thick layers of dust swirled around every time anyone moved, settling everywhere, on the furniture, our food, and our hair. Josh would crawl around in the dust and the debris like a wartime orphan, reaching into the holes in the floorboard and pulling out various prizes which would immediately disappear into his mouth. Meanwhile, I was recovering from my surgery. I weighed eighty-five pounds and couldn't even lift a milk carton. I certainly couldn't pick up Josh. And I felt like shit.

Cash flow ruled my life. Since no one would give me credit, every small amount of growth required cash up front. Our entire savings had gradually been sucked into the business $10,000 at a time. It had become very clear that no bank was going to loan money to this business. My favorite banker response was "We can loan you $50,000 if you can secure the loan with a $50,000 cash balance in your account." Let me get this straight. If I give you $50,000, then you'll loan me $50,000. Sometimes I think I'm in the wrong business.

I was now in my thirties, and it was starting to seem like time was running out. My friends from college had Professions. One of my college roommates called me when she was home visiting her parents. She was a lawyer. She had an Office and a Title and a Salary. Important things. I was so jealous I wanted to puke.

"So how is everything?" I asked.

"Oh my God," she said, "I think my boss is going to take a run for mayor. I'm going to have to decide whether to stay with her or move to another partner."

Poor thing.

I acted nonchalant, as if I made decisions like that all the time.

"Well," I said, "I think you should stay where you are. You'll make more money." Why was I offering bad advice? Had I sunk so low that I was actually discouraging her from an opportunity that might catapult her career forward? Was I afraid she would get even further ahead of me in life?

Luckily she changed the subject.

"My mother sent me an article about Mothers Work. My God, you must be doing great! You know, I have a friend in New York who is an investment banker who specializes in retailing. He's taken lots of companies public." She was really warming up to this idea now. "Do you want to talk to him? Why don't you come up and we'll have lunch with him sometime."

I didn't know whether to laugh or cry. *As if* an investment banker would have the slightest interest in my so-called company. I didn't even have a secretary, for Christ sake. I didn't even have an office. The article she was talking about was just a ridiculous puffed-up piece of self-promotion that some editor who knew someone who knew me cooked up because they needed a story for Mother's Day. The days of the *Wall Street Journal* and *Good Morning America* were long gone. I was just trying to hold on to a little mail-order business that was coasting along doing a few hundred thousand dollars of sales per year.

While I was trying to decide how to retain my dignity while politely turning her down, Josh cruised by me crawling through the streets of Beirut looking for trouble. About twenty feet away from me he stopped and reached into a hole. He pulled out something that to this day I believe was a giant black cockroach. I started gesticulating madly.

"No!" I screamed. "Put it down!"

I knew that in my currently weakened state I would never get to him in time.

He looked up at me with a sweet smile and popped it into his mouth.

"Barbara," I said, "why don't I get back to you on it?"

I don't know which part bothered me the most: the fact that I was so inept as a mother that I couldn't prevent my baby from eating roaches or the fact that my business was going nowhere while my friends were rich professionals who were advancing their careers in good yuppie fashion. I sat there for a long time, my hand resting on the telephone. Tears were running down my face. I silently resolved to sell my business, go back to school, and get a law degree.

After two years of growth in catalog sales, the third year seemed to be going nowhere, even though it seemed like I had done all the right things. I had refined the production of two catalogs per year, fall and spring. I had expanded my advertising to more publications, and learned which ones worked better than others. And I had developed a mix of merchandise that included buying garments from maternity showrooms in New York as well as expanding my own line of suits and dresses which were being manufactured in Philadelphia. Maybe what had seemed like an adventure three years ago was just starting to wear thin. Or maybe I was tired of waiting for future riches beyond my wildest dreams. All I knew was that I wanted my own house now. Grinding out the next catalog didn't have the same thrill as inventing the first one had. Our net sales were going to reach over $300,000 in the third year of business, but after the cost of the merchandise, advertising, and other expenses, there was nothing left. Somehow we were going to have to make a quantum leap if we were going to make this thing successful. And still, just keeping up with our paltry sales level required so much daily grind, we hardly had any energy left to think globally. Even though we could hardly afford it, we decided to hire someone to help us fill the catalog requests and the orders every day.

This was a difficult job to fill. On the one hand, we couldn't afford to pay very much. A part-time person would be nice. On the other hand, we needed someone who could do a little of everything. Someone who was a quick study and who would say the right thing if the *Wall Street Journal* should happen to call for an interview. It seemed like a university might be a place to find someone, so we put a notice on the bulletin boards around Jefferson University, which was just a few blocks away. We found the ideal person in Lena Harris, the wife of a medical student who could only work part-time. She was from the Philippines, and her family was actually in the apparel business.

Dan decided we needed a bigger computer system to automate our daily order entry and fulfillment processes, one that would track sales and inventory, make invoices, and keep a database of our customers. We also wanted to track our advertising better and determine which ones were making money and which ones weren't. By now we had expanded our advertising into a dozen or so publications. We went into all the print media that we thought career women would read. For example, since we had a lot of lawyers as customers, we advertised in the *American Bar Association Journal.* That seemed to work, so then we went into the *CPA Journal,* for accountants. We also advertised in all the women's magazines that had a working slant, like *Working Woman, Working Mother,* and *Savvy Magazine.* And to save money, we designed all the ads ourselves. We found a graphic artist to coordinate all the typesetting and a studio that produced the film exactly to the specification of the magazines and newspapers. We used the heading "Pregnant Executives," and in the bigger ads we would use a picture from the catalog, usually of one of the suits. But what we really needed was a computerized method of tracking every catalog request, and exactly which ad pulled it in, and then which catalog requests turned into orders. That way we could perfect our advertising budget and make it profitable.

"If we're going to grow this business, we have to stay ahead of the technology curve," Dan said. "It will be much harder to switch over to a computer system the longer we wait."

"We can't afford it," I said.

"Beck, we can't afford *not* to. You have to drain the swamp at the same time you're killing the alligators. Otherwise you'll never get ahead. You'll always be stuck in the mire of little operational bullshit. Look how much time we waste counting inventory and keeping track of what sold, and which ads pull. And half the time we don't have the information we need. If we get on-line, we'll know that stuff *instantaneously.*"

Dan was a big believer in technology. I knew he was right.

Of course we needed a better computer system. The little PC we were using was pathetic. It was so slow and limited, it didn't do much more than give our customers the illusion that we were a professional company. But I was dragging my feet because I knew it would mean writing yet another check from our personal bank account. The money Dan got from selling his interest in his computer company was just about gone. I had always thought we could fall back on our savings, but they were disappearing. And the more time that passed, the more unemployable we were both getting, a thought that terrified me. Every check I wrote to the business put us deeper and deeper in the huge hole we were digging for ourselves.

Dan researched in all the mail-order magazines and computer magazines and we finally ended up with a mail-order package of hardware and software that was created by a little company in Ohio, which was in the mail-order business selling bicycle-parts by catalog. They developed their own computer system, which worked so well they decided to start selling the system itself. We liked them because they were small and entrepreneurial like we were, yet they had already sold twenty or thirty of their computer systems, so we were pretty sure they worked. Dan had sold enough computer systems to know that a lot of companies promised more than they ever delivered. The system we bought was a multiuser system with three screens, and room to add three more, and it was driven by a minicomputer, not just a little PC.

Jeff White, the president of the company, came out to install the system. He looked like a hippie. He was about thirty years old, had a beard, and dressed in shorts and a T-shirt. He had actually developed most of the computer system himself—written the computer code and everything. I think his company was the same sort of bootstrap operation that ours was, because he seemed to fit right into our second-floor walk-up makeshift office. He looked around a little and said, "Where can I set up the computer?"

I looked around myself and realized that there was hardly five square feet of empty space in the whole apartment. The entire back room had boxes of catalogs and files and Dan's desk. The middle "living room" was Lena's area and had a little table for lunch. The front room was my office. And our inventory was crammed into every available nook in the office on short rolling racks. Whenever we ran out of space, Dan would hang another long metal electric conduit pipe from little hooks in the ceiling. Since the ceilings in the town house were about twelve feet high, we could walk underneath our inventory. As our company grew we crammed more and more clothes into the ceiling. It looked like dresses floating in the sky. (The clothes, packed in plastic garment bags, had an amazing ability to absorb sound; our office had an eerie muffled silence to it.) When a customer called in with an order, we would simply find the style in the ceiling and look at the hang tag to see if we had the size in stock. We had a couple of broom handles with nails stuck in the end to hook off the items we needed to ship.

Once a week I would make up huge spreadsheets of all the styles and how many of each we had, size by size, and how many I projected we would sell that week and that month. Then we were always running around counting all the styles, because it was so easy to make an adding error or to lose track some other way. It was a terribly simple inventory management system that worked when we started but was becoming impossible to control. Because of Dan's computer advocacy, however, we have always stayed a step ahead of our technology needs. So we have always been ready to grow to the next level, instead of scrambling to catch up after the fact. This became one of our unique strengths. As we expanded our manufacturing and then our retailing scope, our growth was fueled by our use of technology in all areas.

Jeff came up with the solution to the problem of where to put the computer. The bathroom was the only underutilized area in the apartment. The obvious place for the computer was the bathtub. Dan put a board on top of the tub, and Jeff installed the computer right there. They drilled holes through the bathroom wall and Jeff started stringing wires all over the apartment. A terminal in each of the three rooms, and three extra wires in the middle room for future terminals. It took Jeff about two days to get the thing up and running and then he started training us how to use it. I don't believe he ever slept the whole three or four days he spent with us. His eyes just kept getting more and more bloodshot as time went on.

All of us took turns entering data into the computer. We had to type in customers' names and addresses, all the inventory styles with their correct count, and the last month or so of customer orders. It was a royal pain in the ass to get it all input. My mother and I were still typing after midnight that first night. But when we finally finished, the benefit was overwhelming.

When Jeff left, we were totally on-line. Lena could be taking orders on one terminal while my mother was entering in catalog requesters on another one. And I could be printing out invoices and shipping on the third. We had to adapt our systems slightly to fit into the way Jeff's software worked, because we bought an existing package, not a custom one. But we were fortunate that we could fit into it as well as we did. We talked to Jeff by phone an average of three times a day for the next few months while we learned all the intricacies of our new system.

I was confined to the office for almost six months after my back surgery. So while my father ran around to sewing contractors, and Dan did everything else from shooting and printing the new catalog to collecting orders from the post-office box, I was the designated "inside man." It was during this time that in my own humble opinion I became a financial expert. My education and limited work experience involved art, architecture, and engineering. I was always good with numbers, but I had no accounting or business training. I needed a crash course in finance and accounting so I could keep the financial records of the company. Dan gave me his old business accounting workbook that he had used at Harvard Business School, and I learned what debits and credits were. At night he would teach me about finance theory. Things like variable costs versus fixed costs, and gross margin versus net margin. These concepts were like learning hieroglyphics. I was starting from scratch, but I loved learning a new language, and I became the CFO of the company until we grew to the point where we needed to hire one.

It was that call from my friend Barbara that got me thinking about selling our business. If Barbara thought Mothers Work was such a great company, maybe her investment banker friend *could* help us by selling it. I feel like a hypocrite admitting this, since my philosophy is "Never give up!" And yet, I was ready and willing and *dying to* give up. Dan was against the idea. He thought we'd be wasting our time anyway, since the business wasn't turning a profit yet. I thought we could sell it cheap and let someone else turn it around, but Dan was more than financially invested now. He believed in the company and thought we could take it to the next level by working a little harder.

I'll just blame it on my bedraggled physical condition, but I didn't seem to have the energy to try any harder. I wanted more than anything to have a successful business, but did I really want to do what it took to get it? My mother used to tell me, "If it were easy, everyone would do it," but she didn't tell me it would be *this* hard. The thing about being an entrepreneur is that all the hard work is fun if you're moving in a forward direction and winning. It's when you take those backward steps that you realize the only one you have to fall back on is yourself. The grass tends to look greener no matter which side of the corporate/entrepreneur fence you're on. But independence requires self-reliance. And I wasn't at all certain that I could continue to carry the ball on my own any longer, even with Dan there to help me.

I actually found a business broker (yes, in the yellow pages) and met with him and "listed" Mothers Work for sale that year, just as an experiment, or so I told myself. You won't be surprised to learn that we got no action and my little project went nowhere. When your business is so bad that you want to sell it, then trust me, no one wants to buy it. When you stick with it and make it turn around, then you'll get plenty of calls, but you won't want to sell it because you'll recognize the value and the opportunity yourself. Sometimes you just have to stick with it even when you're not sure where it's going, and optimize until that breakthrough event comes about. You can't always wait for luck. You have to create the opportunity.

There are volumes written about companies that were marginal for three, four, even five years, and then took off and became giant companies. For example, Sandra Kurtzig, the founder of a computer programming company named ASK, initially ran her business out of her apartment so she could devote more time to her children. Her big break came four years after she set up shop when one program was picked up by Hewlett-Packard minicomputers. Ultimately ASK became a $400-million company.

Sometimes the big break starts out in a small way and develops over time. The call from Jack Hornsby that we got one morning turned out to be one of those cases. Jack was a tailor in Houston who was looking to expand his business. He had a men's suiting store in a little strip center, and he was trying to expand into women's suits. Remember, back in the early eighties, women's suits that made you look like a man were the rage. Anyway, Jack used to travel to New York once or twice a year to buy fabric and go to the tailors' association meetings, and it was on one of these trips that he spoke with a fabric company salesperson about his new women's business. The subject came around to Mothers Work pretty quickly because that salesperson had just sold us some gray suiting fabric. Jack was the perfect person to understand the need for man-tailored women's maternity business suits. He had lots of customers who needed them! And he was looking for a new product line for his business. It was one of those right-place, right-time convergences that sparked a business opportunity, and the next thing I knew he was standing in our second-floor office. As we hooked clothes down for him to examine, we discussed the idea of his carrying the Mothers Work line of maternity suits in the Hornsby Custom Clothes store.

We reached an agreement: Jack would buy our suits for 50 percent of the retail price listed in our catalog. He had a large initial order, so he could stock up his store and make a real presentation, and after that he could pretty much order as often as he liked and as many items as he needed to fill in whatever he sold. We set his store up in our computer like a mail-order customer, with a wholesale price arrangement. His orders were processed and shipped every day along with all the other mail orders, the only difference being the 50 percent price. We didn't charge him any kind of an up-front fee, and he didn't guarantee any future orders. It was a real free-market kind of an agreement, which would continue only as long as we were both happy with it and the customers showed up to buy the clothes.

We concluded the negotiation in under an hour and sealed it with a handshake. We did follow up later with a "Distributorship Agreement," written by our attorney, but the terms were just a recapitulation of our verbal agreement. I've found that if the fundamentals of a business relationship are good for both parties, and the relationship between the parties is sound, the deal will be a good one. The legal documentation should merely reflect the intent of the two sides. Unfortunately, since the future is impossible to predict, it is important to have an attorney think through the downside of a deal—that is, what happens if things go wrong—so that in the worst case, you are protected. But don't let that drive the basic terms of the agreement.

Jack's order was the largest order for clothes that we had ever gotten. He bought almost a hundred items. And more than that, the future possibilities were exciting. This was going to be our first retail exposure. Who knew where it could lead?

At the same time, we had a very real new challenge in our manufacturing. First of all, we had to accelerate production. Luckily we had built up our inventory enough to fill most of Jack's initial order, but it depleted our stock quite a bit. Second, we had to figure out how to manufacture the line more cost-effectively because obviously our gross margin (the difference between what it cost to make it and the price we sold it) was halved on Jack's order. Usually building up your manufacturing volume drives down your cost at the same time, so we were hoping that the problem would take care of itself—eventually.

By this time we had built up an impressive selection of maternity suits in our catalog. We were also manufacturing a number of dresses and blouses. At first we would just copy the things we had bought in the maternity apparel market in New York, but then I started "designing" new styles. Usually I would go to a store and buy a dress that I thought could be easily adapted to be a maternity style. Then I would hire a patternmaker to make a pattern. Next I would find some fabric. I had a half dozen fabric vendors that sold small quantities of fabric (less than one thousand yards). Burlington fabrics was a good bet for wool suiting fabric, and there were a few manufacturers' reps who would travel around with a suitcase full of fabric samples, good for dresses and blouses. How did we find these people? The usual trial and error and yellow-page chain was still my preferred method. Fortunately Philadelphia has a long history of serving the apparel industry. We were able to find fabric reps, button manufacturers, thread suppliers, and sewing contractors too. All in the yellow pages! We even found a little hole-in-the-wall operation that did nothing but make covered buttons. All you had to do was give them a few yards of fabric and this special kind of plastic button you could buy from Quaker Button Company, and they had these neat little machines that would punch out little fabric circles, and then another little machine that would fold those circles over the plastic button, and *voilà*—a covered button made from the same fabric as your blouse or dress or whatever.

Of course not everything was smooth sailing. Our first experience with patternmaking was a disaster. We had a pretty basic shirt in our first catalog made out of a fabric called a tattersall plaid. It was a big seller in the first catalog, but when we tried to reorder it, we discovered that it had been dropped from the line. Well, I decided right then and there that I would make it myself. I mean, how hard could it be to make a damned shirt? Dan took on the assignment to find fabric. He went to New York one day with several cotton fabric companies in mind and located a great tattersall plaid from Dan River. The only problem was that the minimum order was five thousand yards. At one and a half yards per garment, that would make about 3,300 shirts. But we only needed to make a hundred, and that was pushing it.

Dan took the long view. "The way we're growing, we're going to *need* that much."

"We can't afford it," I said.

Not to mention the fact that we had nowhere to put it. Meanwhile I had located a student at one of the local textile colleges who said she could make a pattern. One night we drove out to her house in northeast Philadelphia and dropped off a sample of the shirt we wanted to reproduce. One week later we picked up the pattern. She charged us $45. We had located a sewing contractor who also had a few cutting tables.

He agreed to produce one hundred shirts for $9 each. He was doing us a big favor to produce such a small lot. We had to supply the fabric, buttons, labels, and a "marker."

"What's a marker?" I asked.

He looked up to heaven. He was probably asking God why he had made the mistake of dealing with such a know-nothing.

"A marker is a long piece of paper with all the pattern pieces drawn on it. You stack up the fabric in big piles and lay the marker on top and then cut out all the pattern pieces."

Shit. Why didn't I know that? "Do you think you could make a marker for me if I give you the pattern?" I asked very sweetly.

"That will cost you extra. And also, I'm going to need a sample before I can start."

I gave him the original shirt that we had copied. I knew I was cutting corners by not testing out the pattern, but I had nobody to make a sample. I wouldn't even know where to begin, and I already had lots of back orders for this shirt. I needed to get it produced now. I just assumed the pattern was an exact reproduction of the shirt we started with.

There was one final thing.

"I'll have the fabric delivered right to your factory," I said. "There might be a little more than you need."

"How much more?" He looked suspicious. "You only need about a hundred and fifty yards."

"A few thousand." I was sort of whispering.

He looked up to heaven again. He shook his head. "That's going to cost you extra," he said.

Two weeks later Dan and I drove back to pick up our hundred shirts. We stuffed them into the trunk of our car, and when we got home we carried them up the stairs in big armfuls, making five or six trips. Dan had two new pipes hanging from the ceiling all ready. The shirts looked great. This was when I was still pregnant with Josh. I decided to put one of them on right then and there because they looked so good. I grabbed a size 4 and pulled it over my head. I stuck my arms through. They wouldn't go. I looked at the cuff. Seemed right, but I couldn't get my hand through it. I unbuttoned the cuff and put my hand through, then tried buttoning it again. No way. I could not button that cuff. It was about an inch too small. Dan started pulling down more shirts, and we checked the cuff sizes. They were all too small! I couldn't even button a size 14 cuff around my wrist. The pattern was just wrong.

Dan and I stared at each other. I didn't know what to do. We had eighteen shirts on back order. We had customers waiting for those shirts. But there was no way we could send out shirts with defective cuffs. I guess the good news was that we had 4,850 yards of fabric left to help with the problem. I called the sewing contractor to discuss the problem, already anticipating his usual refrain. I *knew* this was going to cost me extra.

"Who made this pattern anyway?" he asked. "You better get a patternmaker who knows what the hell he's doing because if your garment doesn't fit, you're screwed before you begin." He had an endearing way of putting it, but actually he was giving me very valuable advice. That was the last time I used a student for patternmaking, and that was the last time I used a pattern that hadn't been tested.

Eventually we had all the cuffs fixed. I had to pay to have every one ripped off, remade, and sewn back on. I lost half of my back orders because my customers got tired of waiting for their shirts. And after all of the "extras" I hardly made any money on those shirts. But once again, I inched forward on the learning curve. Expensive tuition, but valuable lessons.

Before Jack Hornsby came along, our manufacturing skills were greatly improved, but our lots were too small to be meaningful to a sewing contractor. We needed to increase our sales volume even more to be able to order garments in lots of several hundred at a time. It was impossible to "manufacture" fewer than fifty garments. Even one hundred was on the small side. We were ready for Jack's call at the moment he made it. Of course now that we were manufacturing larger lots of garments, in anticipation of future sales, we had to dump even more money into the business to finance the inventory buildup. The more your business grows, the more cash it sucks in. Jack's maternity suit business did better than any of us expected. I flew to Houston for the grand opening. Jack had the *Houston Post* there to do a story, and one of the local TV stations did a thirty-second spot on the evening news. There was clearly a need for our product in Houston.

Dan and I started to seriously think about getting into the retail business in other cities. It was becoming clear that mail order alone could never grow large enough to be profitable. The fundamental flaw in the concept of mail-order maternity clothes was the short-term nature of the customer. It's very expensive to attract a new mail-order customer. You have to spend a lot of money in advertising or in renting lists. So once you get a customer, you need to make her a repeat customer for years afterward. The most valuable asset of a catalog company is its house list. Companies like L.L. Bean and J. Crew are constantly selling more products to the same repeat customers without spending more marketing money. Obviously this whole idea goes out the window when you're dealing with a pregnant woman. Once she has her baby, she's not a customer anymore, so we were constantly spending money to find new customers. To make matters worse, the economics of advertising to pregnant women are awful. A quarter-page ad in the *New Yorker* cost $10,000, yet less than 1 percent of the readers were our target audience. There simply were no magazines directed at only pregnant workingwomen. So our ads were terribly inefficient. The cost per lead was huge. And finally, most pregnant women were just not mail-order shoppers. They wanted to try their clothes on in a store.

We knew that we didn't have the money required to begin opening stores. We also knew we didn't want to simply wholesale our clothes to other maternity stores. We wanted to control the environment our clothes were sold in. Ideally we wanted the stores to be called Mothers Work. We decided to franchise. What did we know about franchising? Nothing. We placed a tiny little classified ad in the maternity trade magazine, called *Maternity Matters,* inviting inquiries about opening a Mothers Work franchised store. I called my lawyer friend Barbara and took her up on her offer to recommend an attorney specializing in franchising. Then we waited for a response to our ad.

Nobody gets it right just coming out of the gate. I mean, my original idea was buying maternity clothes for five and selling them for ten through a mail-order catalog. Now I was making them, not buying them, and I discovered that mail order was fundamentally flawed. I wasn't absolutely sure that franchising was the answer, but in business the important thing is to keep moving ahead. You can study the problem until you're blue in the face, but if you don't take action, you're sure to fail. Ultimately we would find that franchising had its own problems, but for now it beckoned us to follow toward future prosperity.

Getting the Hang of Cash Flow, Credit, Publicity, Technology, Taxes, You Name It

▼ ▼ ▼

Okay. You're in business. You have an idea, you have a product, and you have customers. After the initial rush that comes with simply being in business, you settle into the nuts and bolts of grinding it out every day. Let me give you a few tips about living through the unglamorous daily drudgery. This is the part where a lot of people lose it, because it's just so hard and thankless. But you have to go through this part to get to the glory days.

Cash Flow

Above all, don't run out of cash. You knew that. Now focus on it. You can't win unless you stay in the game. And running out of cash will boot you right out. We know no one will lend you any money, so you have to rely on your own creative financing. Making a profit is always a good place to start. Remember that everything you do is to make a profit. I have seen too many entrepreneurs who get enamored with their product, or the process, or their team of employees and forget why they are in business. Losing money month after month is unacceptable. Change your product or your method of selling it or fire some of your employees, and figure out right away how to make money.

Remember that cash flow and profitability are two different things. Not only do you need to be profitable, but what is infinitely more important is to realize positive cash flow. You might have a fistful of orders for your product, and your accountant might tell you that you have made a big fat profit. But unless you collect the cash quicker than you lay out the money for whatever it takes to deliver that order, you won't have cash flow. And cash flow is the lifeblood of a start-up. Here are a few ways to boost your cash flow.

Buy as much on credit as you can. This may seem obvious, but it took me a while to realize that my vendors would even *give* me credit. Office supplies, fabric, insurance, advertising, you name it. Always try to buy now/pay later, on whatever terms are standard in that industry. Typically that will mean something around thirty days later. When you place your orders, negotiate the payment terms at that time. If your vendors balk at the idea of giving you credit, don't give up. Schedule a meeting with them and go over your financial numbers and your future plans. For example, if they know you have a big new account with an increase in sales coming your way, they may be more inclined to give you credit.

Never give credit if you can help it. Even better, try to get a deposit on future orders. Ship "cash before delivery," meaning they pay *you* before you ship the merchandise. Insist on progress payments. Depending on the nature of your business, you can get creative here. If you are forced to deliver a product first and collect later, then you need to put tremendous resources into collections. Someone on your staff needs to keep track of all money owed to you and be on a regular schedule of making calls to collect it. (This might be you if you're just starting.) Your customer has your money! Go get it.

Lease, don't buy. This may cost more in the long run, but in the short term it will save cash. For example, if you go out and buy a new copier and pay cash, it might cost you $2,500 right away, all at once. If you lease it over three years, your payments would be $83.05 per month, including the 12 percent interest you pay. Over three years' time, you would pay $2,989.80, which is obviously more than the $2,500 you would pay in cash. But *you're not out the $2,500 on the first day.* You can use that money for something else: more inventory, hiring someone, or growing your business in some other way. And two or three years from now if your business has grown, those $83.05-per-month payments will be much easier to make because your revenue will be higher every year. Automobiles, office equipment, etc.—whenever possible, lease it or rent it.

Don't use consultants. In the first place, you can't afford it. Don't hire a consultant to figure out how to make your company profitable, or to do a marketing survey, or to find an investor, or to deliver any other "soft" product. It's your job to make your company profitable, study the market, and find investors. When you are starting up, all the scrappy things you do, the million innovative ways you save money and find new opportunities for new revenue, are happening at lightning speed. You will react to them and create new opportunities by doing things and being there. A consultant will be talking to you on a much more theoretical level, and while he might have some inspirational or general advice, he won't help you with the day-to-day minutiae that will determine whether your business lives or dies.

Cultivate the media and publicity. If your business sells a consumer product, good publicity is invaluable. You couldn't afford the equivalent amount of advertising that an article in the lifestyle section of your local paper is worth. Not only does publicity get your company's name out, it does it in a way that endorses it with the goodwill of the medium itself. Another benefit of publicity is in connection with raising capital. When you go to the bank or try to get venture capital, it sure is nice to include an article about your company in your package. Since as a small business you probably don't have the budget to hire a PR agency, much of the workload falls on your shoulders.

The most important principle to remember when generating publicity is to be "newsworthy." Editors and journalists are trying to sell newspapers and they need interesting stories to do it. They don't want a boring exposition about the merits of your product. They want a funny or interesting or memorable anecdote about how you started your company. Or a new survey about how many multiple births occurred in your city last year, driving the need for your new stroller designed for triplets. Don't waste your time and money sending out a press release announcing your new catalog unless it is surrounded with an interesting, newsworthy story that goes with it.

The press release is your best method for communicating to the press. It should be one page long, or, if it is longer than that, it should have a succinct, one-page introduction. The subject of your press releases can be whatever you think will attract an editor's attention. If your company is brand-new and addresses a unique consumer need, then that alone could generate a good press release. If you have nothing new, try to generate news. For example, a survey is always great media fodder. Take your own survey and publish the results. You might survey your customers' buying habits, their demographics, or their opinions. "First-time mothers are nursing their babies 65 percent of the time, according to our recent survey. This is a complete reversal from just one decade ago." Or "Mary's Exotic Tea Boutique surveyed five thousand consumers and found that tea drinking in this country is preferred over coffee by 43 percent of all consumers under the age of twenty-five. What does this mean for the future of the coffee industry in America?" Whatever your press release covers, just remember that it must be *newsworthy.* Ask yourself: "Would I want to read this in the paper?"

Send your press release to as many places as you can think of. You can use the straightforward method of buying your targeted magazine or newspaper and then sending your release to the editors that you think would be most interested in your topic. Put their name on the envelope, preferably handwritten. And for the most important media send your release by an overnight service so it has a sense of urgency and stands out from the clutter. Then follow up with telephone calls, offering to expand on the release or to answer any questions they have. You may or may not get through, but you'd be surprised how many reporters and editors answer their own phones. And don't forget the local TV news stations and talk shows.

Generating publicity takes a lot of time, but just one hit can make the payback worthwhile. And publicity begets more publicity. So once you succeed, your results can snowball. Even a small article in a local newspaper might be read by the editor of a larger paper or magazine. Timing can be critical in publicity. An editor might like your story, but not have room for it at a given moment. Keep on generating more press releases on new events or new angles. Sooner or later your hard work will intersect with opportunity.

Pay your taxes and licenses. Not only are government fees of all sorts expensive, but the red tape you have to go through to fill out forms and pay them is enough to make you crazy. Nevertheless, you need to figure out how to get through the maze and pay up. Payroll taxes, sales taxes, business permits, business privilege taxes, building occupancy fees . . . I could go on forever. You probably need to check with your accountant to be sure you have identified all of your obligations and are paying them. You may think you don't want to know about all the taxes and fees, but believe me, they will find you eventually, and then you'll be subject to back fees, penalties, interest, and even nastier things. This is not the place to save cash.

If you're in a bind, string out another vendor. But *don't* get behind on your payroll tax withholding payments. You can't run your business from jail.

Sell something you never knew you had. Like your brand name. License it to a related product company. Or your expertise. Go on the lecture circuit or become a consultant on the side (to someone who hasn't read this book). Or sell a franchise. Or cook up a joint venture with a big company. They have cash, and you have entrepreneurial drive. A good combination.

Hiring and Firing and Managing Employees

Entrepreneurs are famous for being lousy managers of people. They tend to want to do it all themselves. They're short-tempered and impatient. They're not people-oriented, they're results-oriented. And when cash is short, you can't compete with the big salaries and benefits that big companies offer their employees. Yet you need talented people if you're going to grow.

Remember, you *do* have something to offer that big companies don't: challenge and opportunity. For the kind of driven, creative person that you're looking for, being stuck in a mature no-growth company with a dead-end job is like death. The kind of spark plugs you're looking for value an atmosphere of fast-paced action with unlimited opportunity. Learn to market what you have. When you are interviewing candidates, be a salesperson for your company and convey your enthusiasm and hopes for the future.

The other thing you can offer employees is flexibility. I was always able to attract smart people who didn't quite fit into the nine-to-five world for various reasons. Mothers with young children who needed flextime. Students who couldn't work regular hours and lacked experience, but made up for it with boundless energy and drive. And sometimes, people who just had weak résumés, such as immigrants who couldn't speak great English or physically challenged individuals who had a difficult time fitting into mainstream America. The great thing about a start-up is that results are the only thing that matters. My company was always a crazy quilt of multinational, varied-background people who had a lot to offer and who flourished in a fast-paced no-rules kind of company.

As your company grows, you will need different kinds of employees. As sad as it is, the person who does well in a five-person entrepreneurial start-up may not be happy or productive when your company grows into a larger workforce with a little more bureaucracy and structure. Somewhere along the line she will leave or you will fire her. It may be better for both of you. Don't grieve too much. Just move on. At each stage of development you have to recognize what your company's needs are. And do what's right for the whole organization.

Never hire secretaries or assistants unless your company sells a service that requires a fancy office where customers take away their first impression, and you have to type up a lot of professional reports for them. Otherwise, with voice mail and cheap personal computers, there is no need for assistants. They will only create memos and bureaucracy. My company is a $300-million-revenue enterprise today, and we still don't have a single secretary. We type our own letters and memos (which really minimizes that activity) and we answer our own phones.

Computer Systems and Technology

I have never made an investment in computer systems and technology that didn't pay off. However, be sure that you are investing in "appropriate" technology. For example, you do not need a fancy computer inventory control system for one store. But when you get to three, then start to think about it. It's a tough call to know when the payoff will kick in. This is the one area where you might make an exception and hire a consultant if you are not technologically oriented. You might need help in determining the right computer system, and considering the amount of time, energy, and money you're going to spend, you better make sure it's the right one. Think about how much money you pay one employee in a year—$15,000? $20,000? Now think about how many employees you won't have to hire if you get the right computer system. The math usually works out in other areas of your business too. Voice mail systems, automated production systems, and other technology aids have a high payback. And usually you can lease them, which is good for your cash flow.

Accountants and Lawyers

I recommend that you bring in a good accountant and attorney as soon as you can. The first time I had our accounting records reviewed I learned many things that I had been recording erroneously. I was actually more profitable than I realized, and obviously when you are trying to attract a bank loan or investor, you want to show a history of profitability. Your accountant will also make sure you are paying all the taxes and fees you need to.

You also want to have an attorney review your major contracts and other legal documents. I'm not saying you should go overboard here, but without running up a huge legal bill, you can save yourself lots of agony later. If your professionals believe in the future of your business, they may cut you a break on fees in your first few years, hoping to build a relationship with you for when you have a bigger, more successful company. I even paid one of my early-on attorneys about two years of legal fees by giving him some equity in the company.

Without question, the best way of finding a good accountant, lawyer, or other professional is through referral. Ask people you know. Interview your professionals' other clients and see if they're absolutely happy with them. I actually found one of my attorneys when he represented the other side in a transaction we were doing. We thought he did such a good job representing the *other* side that we fired our lawyer and hired him (after the transaction was complete).

They say that God lives in the details. In a start-up the details can kill you if you don't manage every one of them. You're driving yourself crazy running around worrying about every nickel-and-dime thing that comes along because there's no one to delegate to. And every dollar that is squandered is *your* dollar. It's not like the big companies, where you can take the pencils home and nobody notices. Or lose a few dollars because you didn't take the time to negotiate the lowest bid on the construction of your new store. That's the nature of a start-up. Everything matters, and it's all up to you. So don't run out of cash. And don't run out of patience. Better days are coming.

Chapter Five Checklist

▾ Cash flow is the lifeblood of a start-up.

▾ Buy as much on credit as you can. Or buy now, pay later.

▾ Never give credit if you can help it. Ship cash before delivery.

▾ Lease, don't buy—even if it costs more in the long run.

▾ Good publicity is invaluable. Moreover, publicity begets more publicity.

▾ Don't get behind on payroll tax payments or other taxes or fees. It can put you out of business.

▾ You need talented employees if you are to grow. Offer them opportunity and flexibility in lieu of high salaries.

▾ Computers and technology can help you run your company more effectively and efficiently.

▾ Hire a good accountant and attorney as soon as you are able.

▾ God lives in the details—and in a start-up, they can kill you if you don't manage every one.

chapter six

Franchising Takes Us Forward

Meryl Goldsmith answered our ad. She wanted to open the first Mothers Work franchised store in New York, and she was the perfect candidate. She was a buyer for Federated Department Stores who had risen to a high level and was tired of corporate life and ready to open her own retail boutique. She was married to a successful entrepreneurial guy named Mike, who had made a killing in real estate in Manhattan. They had the financial wherewithal and entrepreneurial bent to start a new business. Meryl knew more about fashion and retailing by far than we did, and I almost felt like we should pay her for opening the first franchise. She had really studied the market in Manhattan for fashion boutiques and had already concluded that opening just another women's clothing store would be financial suicide. She knew she needed a special niche within women's fashion, and she had just about concluded that maternity might be the answer. That was when she saw our little ad in *Maternity Matters* magazine and called us.

Meryl and Mike took the train down that weekend to meet us. The minute I saw Meryl I knew I could work with her. She was about my age, all dressed in black, very New York. She had a nervous tic which made her blink her eyes all the time, which I took as a good sign of a workaholic. We struck a deal sitting in my mother's greenhouse on the first floor. My mother served chocolate chip cookies and kept Isaac and Josh more or less out of the way.

By this time the inventory had leaked into the spare bedroom in the basement of my mother's apartment (formerly my bedroom). Like a creeping vine, it was slowly taking over the entire house. All the furniture was pushed against the wall in my old bedroom, with the bed up on its side to make more room. There were racks and racks jammed in, full of clothes. It was overwhelming. We walked Mike and Meryl all over the house showing them different styles. Meryl was really excited and ready to get going.

The basic concept of the franchise was similar to the deal we had struck with Jack Hornsby. Meryl would buy Mothers Work clothes from us at 50 percent of the retail price in the catalog and sell them in her store, which would be called Mothers Work. We would license the Mothers Work name to her and give her the exclusive right to carry the Mothers Work line in her territory, which was the New York region. We also gave her the rights to develop stores later on in New York State, Connecticut, and northern New Jersey. In exchange, she agreed to pay us 1.5 percent of all of her sales, as a royalty payment. My attorney had told me that typical royalty payments in a franchise arrangement could be anywhere from

1 percent to 10 percent. Since we were brand-new and Meryl was taking a big risk and helping us grow our business, we decided to keep the royalty small. But we all agreed that if her sales exploded and exceeded $500,000, then the royalty on sales over $500,000 would be 2.5 percent, and if by some miracle her sales exceeded $1 million, then the royalty on those sales over $1 million would be 3.5 percent.

We all thought that Meryl's store should be right in midtown Manhattan, where the largest number of working women were found. But we doubted that she could afford to pay the exorbitant rents that were paid by retailers in that area and still make a profit. A thousand-square-foot space, which would be a little on the small side, could easily cost $300,000 or $400,000 per year.

"Career maternity clothes are a destination product," Dan said. "You can be upstairs, or behind a lobby, and your customers will find you. As long as you are close to where they work. I just don't think you have to pay for prime street space. After all, this product is unique. There's nowhere else to buy it."

Mike was the negotiator. "How do we know our customers won't just order from the catalog? Are you still going to send catalogs to women in Meryl's territory?"

Of course I was. I had my *own* business to think about too. I couldn't let the mail-order business decrease in exchange for a 1.5 percent royalty on what Meryl sold in New York. "How about if we print the name and address of Meryl's store right on the front of the catalog?" I suggested. "That way it will actually be a form of marketing for you. People would *rather* shop in a store than by catalog. So if they know we have a store in New York, they'll go there." I figured that was a good compromise. Maybe some of them would still order by mail. After all, who had time to shop?

We worked through the contract terms in a give-and-take fashion, with both parties eager to make it work. How big was the territory? How much local advertising would they do? How much national advertising would we do? Meryl wanted to carry other lines of maternity clothes in her store. She had already visited some of the maternity showrooms in New York, including Betty Bailey and Mr. Kent, and she wanted to carry casual maternity clothes, like jeans and tees, as well as Mothers Work career clothes. "Why should they shop anywhere else?" she said. We agreed as long as we would get a royalty on those sales too. And as long as she agreed to always carry 85 percent of the Mothers Work line as represented in the catalog. That way we knew our clothes would be sold in a territory that would now be unavailable to ourselves. Now that we were giving the exclusive rights to Meryl to open Mothers Work stores in New York, we could never open stores ourselves there, or sell wholesale to any other stores in her territory. We were counting on Meryl to do a good job for us. Not all franchise contracts have the concept of exclusive territories. Just think about how many McDonald's hamburger restaurants there are and how close to each other they can be. But we were willing to give exclusive territories to Mothers Work franchises because the market for career maternity clothes was so small. We didn't think anyone would buy a franchise if they weren't guaranteed to have all the business in a large area around their store.

When they left late that evening, we all shook hands and then hugged each other. We had worked out all the major issues, and now we would have our first Mothers Work store.

It was a turning point in our development, and once again it seemed like we had a future. Miraculously, one week later, we both signed the official franchise contract. Meryl sent her signed copy back to us with her first order for merchandise and a check. It was like manna from heaven. Her order was for more than three hundred items, and the check was for the whopping amount of $15,000. We immediately scrambled around to see what we had and what we didn't. Between Meryl's orders and Jack Hornsby's, we were going to have to dramatically increase our rate of production. And it was clear that we were just plain out of room to store any more clothes. We decided it was time to find a warehouse for our inventory.

Philadelphia was the garment center of the country back in the late 1800s, early 1900s. We still have a "garment district," which is next to Chinatown and borders what we used to call skid row. There are hundreds of loft buildings that used to house thriving garment factories and are perfectly designed for that use—large open spaces with a freight elevator and stairwell in one corner. Of course, at that point in time, they were mostly dirty and dingy, and the neighborhood wasn't the greatest, but they fit our purpose. And they were available, not to mention dirt-cheap. We gave my father the assignment of locating a ten-thousand-square-foot loft space in the garment district. He found it on the fifth floor of an amazingly crappy building at 12th and Arch Streets. The rent was $2.50 per square foot per year. We could afford this, but just barely.

It took us three straight days to move all the inventory out of our house. If you have ever seen those clowns in the circus that keep climbing out of the Volkswagen, and you can't imagine how they ever got so many of them in there in the first place, then you can get an idea of what the process was like. The neighbors were incredulous. If they had had any idea of how many garments we had in our house, I'm sure someone would have called the fire marshal. Or the zoning commission. Or any other government regulatory body, since I'm sure we broke every rule. We had a part-time girl named Natalie whom we had hired a few months prior to pick up clothes from contractors. She had just gotten back from Israel, where she was living with her boyfriend. She was sort of a freewheeling type and loved being involved in our crazy company. She drove a huge old Buick around and she would stuff all the clothes in her trunk and drive them back to our house. Half of the time the trunk didn't actually close, so garments and plastic bags would be whipping in the wind behind her as she tore around. She had this way of pulling headfirst into a parking spot on our block so that her big old Buick was diagonally parked, as opposed to parallel parked, the back half sticking into the street. Then she'd grab armloads of clothes and start hauling them up the steps.

We must have made a thousand and one trips driving garments the twenty or so blocks to the new warehouse, finishing up at around eleven Sunday night. We were all exhausted and aching. As usual, our efforts were replete with miscalculations, including how many clothes there were and how many racks we needed. Plus my father had found a cheap source of used racks that really weren't the right kind. They were for store displays, as opposed to warehouse or manufacturers' racks, and they were too short, and impossible to move around. Finally, in our exhaustion, we threw the garments in big piles on the floor. It took us weeks afterward to find everything and get it hung up and organized.

When we finally finished up that night, we collapsed in my mother's living room. Isaac and Josh had fallen asleep on my parents' bed. We all just stared at each other in a daze.

"We need to buy a van," Dan said. "We can't be dragging these clothes around in car trunks anymore."

My father was nodding. I was too tired to say, "We can't afford it." It wasn't fair. Every time we got ahead a little, new urgent needs popped up that claimed our rewards. Between the warehouse and the increase in inventory that we needed, we were further behind the cash eight ball than ever. I still didn't make even a dime of salary! The business just couldn't afford it. I went to bed feeling sorry for myself. The worst part was I couldn't quit now even if I wanted to. We had new obligations. We had to keep going. God only knew where it would lead.

Life was different now that we had the clothes out of our house. It was great to have the space back, but now my routine included going to the warehouse almost every day. Of course we needed more help too. Gradually our payroll was expanding. We needed order pickers and order-entry clerks. I hired a student from a local junior college to help keep the books and write checks. My mother kept the payroll records and wrote the paychecks. All told, we had eight or nine employees now. Learning how to manage them was all new for me.

I will never forget the first weekend we finally decided to take a day off and drive down to Atlanta, where Dan's parents lived. We bundled the two boys up and hit the highway on an early Friday morning. My parents were minding the shop for the one business day of our extended weekend. We hadn't had a vacation since Isaac was born, and surely they could keep things under control for one day. Sometime around four we stopped and called home to see how everything was going.

"Thank God you called!" My mother was frantic. I was afraid the place had burned down or something. "It's Friday and you left without signing the paychecks!"

"Oh, for crying out loud. Is that all? I'll pay them on Monday when we get back." I mean, *come on.* Is that all the dedication they have? I hadn't drawn a single paycheck for myself and they're complaining about getting paid one day late?

"Beck, I don't think that's going to work," my mother said. "They're all just standing around waiting upstairs. Natalie says her rent check will bounce if she doesn't get paid today."

"Well, can't you deal with it somehow?" Some vacation. Driving for ten hours in a van with two screaming babies and now this.

"I guess I can run to the bank and get cash . . ." She was sighing now. A clear sign of her disapproval. "The payroll is almost two thousand dollars. I don't know if I have that much in my account."

"Well, get as much as you can! I'll pay you back on Monday." I looked at my watch. It was 4:15. "You better hurry. The bank is going to close."

She sighed again. But she did bail me out of that tight spot like many other rescue operations she performed. I had a lot to learn. For starters, I learned that I couldn't mess around with someone's paycheck. Employees are not owners. They may be dedicated and they may be great workers, but when the ship comes in, they will not be sailing away into the sunset with you. And they know that. I didn't realize it then, but I know now that it is the highest level of disrespect and arrogance to expect someone to sacrifice their current payback for your future rewards. I had a deal with my employees that I hadn't acknowledged: help me now and I will pay you. It was incumbent upon me to honor that bargain.

Meryl found a location for her Manhattan store on 57th Street between Fifth and Sixth Avenues. It was on the fifth floor of a small building filled primarily with art galleries and the rent was only $45,000 per year. She had no street sign or presence of any kind, but it was truly ground zero for workingwomen. We had a plan to build up her customer awareness by distributing the latest version of the Mothers Work catalog in nearby obstetricians' offices. She manually stickered each catalog with the name, address, and grand-opening date of the new store. Then she pounded the pavement, leaving stacks of fifty or so catalogs in each doctor's waiting room. There couldn't be a more direct way of reaching pregnant women at the beginning of their term. By the time her store opened she had scores of pregnant women salivating. She did $10,000 on the first Saturday. Women had to wait in line to get into a dressing room. Somehow they all found her up there on the fifth floor. And she wasn't even listed in the yellow pages yet, which we learned later was the absolute number one draw in her marketing program. That first call from Jack Hornsby just a few short months prior was developing into a whole new area of growth for Mothers Work.

Washington, D.C., was the second franchise. It came right on the heels of Meryl's store. Three women partners contacted us. One was a lawyer, one was a store manager for one of the big department stores in D.C., and one worked for her family's business. They all had recently been pregnant, and

Suzanne, the store manager, saw our ad in the *New Yorker* that had the "Inquire about opening a franchise in your area" tag line. We decided to charge them an up-front fee of $10,000. There really is no right amount for an initial franchise fee. Again, my attorney had enough experience with franchises to advise us on a range of typical fees charged by smaller companies like ours. He felt that $10,000 was on the low side, and $30,000 was the high end. We also raised the ongoing royalty percent. Now that we knew the concept worked, we were in a stronger position. Suzanne negotiated the deal for the group. When she balked about the fees, we threw Baltimore into their territory. That sealed the deal. The Washington, D.C., "troika," as I fondly thought of them, latched onto the obstetrician marketing program like fiends. All three distributed that catalog like crazy. We sold them the catalog at a small markup and made money on every catalog they distributed. They were driving down to Virginia and practically up to Delaware leaving stacks of catalogs in every obstetrician's office they could find. Of course it paid off in their grand opening. Following Meryl's example, they located right downtown, in the back of a lobby of an office building. I took the train down for the first day, and Suzanne had invited every newspaper and local evening news reporter you could imagine to cover the opening. It was a huge success: $14,000 on day one, topping Meryl.

We were on a roll. The success of the franchise business didn't escape Lena's attention. From the day we had hired her as our first employee, she had observed our progress. She was on the front lines taking orders and witnessing up close the success that these women were having even though they had no experience in running a store or selling maternity clothes.

It seemed like a sure thing. She came to me and asked if she could buy the Philadelphia franchise. She had it all worked out. Her father was going to bankroll it and she had a little space picked out in a downtown office building. My reaction was mixed. On the one hand, I didn't want to lose her. She had worked out to be the perfect employee. The idea of finding a replacement for her and then training that person made me weary. Lena knew all the ins and outs of our computer system and our product line. On the other hand, we were anxious to keep building stores as quickly as possible, and Lena would make a perfect franchisee. Lena had a friend named Rhonda that she thought would make a great replacement for herself. She really *had* thought of everything.

In the end, the benefit of another up-front franchise fee won out. In order to rationalize the up-front fee, we devised a formula that tied the fee to the population of the territory in question. So the bigger the territory, the more you paid for it. It was a commonsense formula that Dan and I devised, using the Rand McNally book of metropolitan regions, defined by zip codes, with population statistics for every zip code area. We included a copy of the relevant map and population data as an exhibit right in the contract. We charged Lena $10 per thousand in population, making the Philadelphia territory worth more than $25,000, which was about the amount that we had independently decided the Philadelphia territory was worth. But now we had a formula for future contracts.

Franchising was turning out to be a gold mine for us. Every initial franchise fee was like found money. There was virtually no expense or cost of goods associated with it. It was like that Green Stamp business Dan had tried to get me to start. Self-financing. The only thing was that every new franchise left a trail of new business needs in its wake. More inventory. More order taking. More accounting. We were constantly stretched thin by our growing business. Which led us to sell more franchises, which led to a need for more infrastructure. It was a vicious cycle.

Our new warehouse was filling up with inventory. Jeff White had flown out for a few days and set us up with a couple of remote terminals and printers at the warehouse which were connected by modem back to the main computer in our house. Every morning we would send over the prior day's orders from the house to the warehouse so they could be shipped out. First a pick list would be printed, then, when all the orders were packed and checked, the invoices would print. The finished shipping information plus any new inventory receipts from sewing contractors would then be modemed back to the main computer, and the perpetual inventory records in the main computer would be updated. Theoretically the computer would have an accurate record of every garment in the warehouse at the end of every day. Once a month we would take a physical count of all the inventory and compare it to the computer records to make sure the computer was accurate. We needed to make certain that the data and the inventory meshed. If you send a size 12 customer a size 6 dress, you have a recipe for an unhappy customer.

About two or three months after we moved into the warehouse the physical counts started to diverge from the computer records. We would correct the computer inventory after every physical count so that we would start the month with a correct computer inventory. Then the next month it would diverge again. At first it was minor. Then it got bigger. All of a sudden, managing our inventory had become difficult. It wasn't hanging in our house anymore. People walked in and out of the warehouse all day long. And half the time Dan and I weren't even there. Anybody could grab a few things. Or put stuff in a box and ship it to themselves. Or wear something home under their coat. We had to face the fact that someone was stealing. I tried to analyze the missing items. Was it all one size, which might mean one person was taking it for herself? Or was it size runs, which might mean someone was reselling it to a store? Was it recent deliveries? Maybe one of the contractors was short-shipping us, or maybe the van driver was skimming off the top when he made his deliveries. But I couldn't find a pattern. Maybe someone was coming in after hours and taking things. We had a lock on the door, but we didn't have an alarm system. And several people had keys to the warehouse.

I was learning that a business that has both inventory and employees has a recipe for "shrink," which is just a polite way of saying unexplained loss of inventory. It could be outright theft by employees, it could be sloppy record keeping, or it could be lack of security, allowing other related individuals, like delivery people and salespeople, to steal. And the last thing in the world you want to do, as a business manager, is just accept it. You have to constantly fight it and beat it down. You have to devise security systems that uncover theft. You have to improve your record keeping so that you have an accurate count of your inventory at all times, and you can immediately detect shrink. And you have to create a bond with your employees so that they are your partners in the business, and your partners in preventing shrink. Finally, if all else fails and you discover fraud or theft of any kind, you have to make that grounds for immediate termination. You simply cannot tolerate shrink, or you will allow your company to develop a culture that works against you.

The third month was the worst physical count we took. There were almost a hundred garments missing. That was almost $5,000 of merchandise in one month. We couldn't just keep bleeding. This was more than an employee wearing a garment home or stuffing one in his or her bag. This was much more serious. One week later we took another physical inventory. We had lost *another* $1,500. No more analyzing. We had to put a stop to it.

"Someone is stealing after hours. That's all there is to it," I said. It was four in the afternoon and we had just finished our physical inventory. Either Dan or I had been at the warehouse every single minute since the first-of-the-month inventory. Neither one of us saw anything suspicious going on. The only way we could have lost that much in one week's time was during the night when the premises were vacated.

Dan was thinking it over. "We need an alarm," he said. "One where only we have the combination."

"Maybe Leon can work on it tomorrow."

"No, we need it now. Today. Right away." He was getting all agitated. "Beck, we're losing $1,500 a week. And now that we've stirred everything up, whoever is stealing knows we're onto them. They might decide to take a whole lot before we get an alarm in. We could lose *thousands of dollars* tonight."

"Well, there's no way we can get an alarm installed today. It's already four. How about a guard service?"

All the employees were wandering around aimlessly while Dan and I were figuring out what to do. *Who was taking this stuff?* Suddenly everyone looked suspicious: the head order picker was slinking around, trying to look busy. Another employee was looking guilty while straightening out the hangers. I got absolutely nowhere calling around to guard services. I called half a dozen, looking them up in the yellow pages. Nobody could do anything on such short notice. Dan ran out to Radio Shack and got a cheap little alarm that could be installed on the front door. He finished installing it by about 6:30 that night, cursing the whole time. We finally drove the van home to dinner, which my steadfast mother had waiting for us.

"That dipshit alarm isn't going to do anything," Dan said over chicken noodle soup. "All it does is ring. It doesn't call the police. It doesn't call us. And what if they come up the back fire stairs?"

I didn't know what to say. He was right. But what could we do?

"I'll call Robinson Alarm Company in the morning," my father said. "They should be able to install a system the same day."

"That isn't good enough," Dan screamed. "We could lose *everything* tonight."

We all stared at him.

"I'm going back over there." He had a deliberate calm now. "I'm sleeping there tonight." He stood and went upstairs.

"I don't think that's such a good idea." My mother was whispering. Why did she always whisper at times like this?

I knew when Dan was serious, and I knew there was no talking him out of this ridiculous idea. What if someone came in with a gun? What was he really going to do? Was $1,500 of inventory worth risking his life?

Dan came downstairs carrying a sleeping bag and a huge crowbar.

"What the hell do you think you're going to do with that thing?" This was getting out of hand. He didn't answer me. He was just heading out the front door.

"Will you drive me over?" he asked, more a challenge than a question.

I grabbed my bag. "Put the kids in bed," I yelled over my shoulder to my mother as I ran out the door.

We drove over in stony silence. As we pulled up to the warehouse a huge rat ran across our path. In the steamy summer Philadelphia night, the smells of nearby Chinatown wafted into the deserted street.

"Are you sure you want to do this?" I gave it one last feeble attempt.

Dan leaned over and gave me a kiss as he got out of the van. "If I don't make it, I'm leaving you my share of the inventory."

"That's not funny." I watched him disappear into the warehouse. What a monumentally stupid idea this was. I should have never let him do it. On the other hand, he was impossible to stop once he believed in something. That was why I married him. I sighed and started home.

I won't keep you in suspense. Nothing happened that night, besides two very worried entrepreneurs getting very little sleep. Every time I heard a siren go by I woke up and worried. For his part, Dan had barricaded himself inside the fifth floor, wedging big hunks of wood into the door handle. He slept with the crowbar next to him. But we didn't lose any inventory.

We had our real alarm system put in the next day, and our

shrink was reduced to a manageable level. I never did determine whether someone was stealing or not, and ever since we moved the inventory out of our house we have never been able to eliminate shrinkage completely. That steamy night years ago was our initiation into the management of shrink.

We left the year 1984, three years after I started the business, with franchises in Houston, New York, Philadelphia, and D.C., as well as a dozen or so serious inquiries about franchising in other cities. For the first time in a long time, I felt like Mothers Work was moving in a forward direction. The initial franchise fees were like an investment in the company, and the resulting growth was there. The funny thing was that in the midst of the growth, we were sowing the seeds of our future calamity. By the time we had the funds, and the will to open our own retail locations, we had sold every major metropolitan area in the country to franchisees as exclusive territories. And after the initial growth spurt, the franchisees simply stopped expanding. But that realization was months, even years, away. In the meantime, life was getting better, and the future looked rosy.

Everything You Need to Know About Franchising but Didn't Know Whom to Ask

▼ ▼ ▼

Some of the largest, most successful businesses in the world are franchised. McDonald's comes to mind immediately. Usually more established, tested businesses are the candidates for franchising, but not always. I guess we were an extreme case, because when we franchised Mothers Work stores, we had no prototype store at all to model. The benefit of franchising is that you leverage your own talents and money with those of other motivated entrepreneurs who essentially become your business partners. Franchising can be a very quick way to grow a business. But it can also be a double-edged sword if your "partners" develop different ideas about growing the business than you have. After all, they will have invested a considerable amount of time and money into the business and they will want some say in the direction of the business. Investing in a good lawyer to write a strong contract is a good idea, but ultimately, as in all business relationships, it boils down to two people being able to work together. It is worth the time to get to know each potential franchisee and develop the confidence that you agree on the fundamentals of your business before you sign them up. If you decide to franchise, you will need quite a bit of legal advice, but here I will give you some commonsense practical considerations based on my experience of franchising Mothers Work.

What Is a Franchise?

A franchise is a business relationship between a company that has a product or service for sale (the franchiser) and a person or company who licenses that product or service to do business using the franchiser's trademarks, brands, and methods (the franchisee). The franchiser usually provides management training and a proven method of doing business to the franchisee. The franchisee agrees to follow the guidelines set out by the franchiser, and pays a continuing series of fees called royalties for the rights of being a franchisee. Usually the franchisee agrees to purchase supplies and inventory from the franchiser. The idea is to take a successful small business, such as a retail store or professional service, and duplicate that concept around the country, or even the world, churning out new locations like a cookie cutter. The franchisee gets the benefit of owning his or her own business with a substantial portion of the start-up risk taken out of the equation—namely, the overall marketing viability of the concept. And since we live in a brand-driven economy, the advantage of opening a McDonald's hamburger restaurant as opposed to Mary Ellen's Hamburger Restaurant is obviously enormous. Plus, the franchiser's ongoing marketing and advertising budget will far exceed that of a single individual as a new start-up. In our franchise contracts we agreed to do a minimum dollar amount of national advertising and to list the franchise store address and city on the front of every catalog we produced. The benefit to us, as the franchiser, was expanding quickly with the help of other entrepreneurs.

Advantages and Disadvantages of Franchising Your Business

The biggest advantage of franchising is the ability to expand your business quickly without a lot of capital. Every entrepreneur who wants to grow his or her business comes up against the need for capital. If your business is good and you are patient, there is nothing like using retained earnings to grow the business. But if you're in a hurry, if you think it's a "grow or die" situation before the competition wins the market share, then you must grow to make money and stay in the game. This was one of the reasons we decided to franchise. We were motivated to grow quickly because we felt the market for career maternity clothes was a new opportunity that we wanted to take advantage of before anyone else did. We wanted to get there first and establish a national presence with brand awareness. Franchising did that for us. Your franchisees are not only managers of your new locations, they are your partners and fellow business owners. Hopefully they, too, are in it for the long run. They won't quit when the going gets rough. They won't steal the merchandise when you're not there. They will work their tails off and creatively try to make the business a success. In a young growth business, human capital is equally as important as the financial. Franchising provides both.

Of course nothing comes without strings attached. If the biggest advantage of franchising is the addition of entrepreneurs into your business, then it is also the biggest disadvantage. They don't work for you. You have to remember: they work for themselves. As long as business is good and all the franchisees are dancing to the same tune, things are fine. But the day might come when one or some of your franchisees don't like some particular aspect of how you are running the business. They may develop their own ideas. They may be unhappy about the marketing/advertising campaign you are running. One of them may be a weak manager and lose money, which he or she may try to pin on your actions. All of these things can be worked through, but they are challenging. And you are bound to your franchisees by your contract. Like a marriage, it may be hard to disentangle.

If you decide to franchise your business, you will accelerate its growth, but you will not be the sole beneficiary of that growth. Of course this is the consequence of using any form of outside capital. Equity investors will share in the ultimate value of the company. Banks and other debt investors will require interest and ultimately a return of principal. Even your mother will want to get paid back! Unless you have enough money to fund your own growth, and few of us scrappy entrepreneurs do, you will probably be inviting others into your business in some form.

One further consideration of franchising your business is

the legal and accounting complexity it will add. The primary disadvantage is the time and money required to manage it. But I wouldn't let this factor alone discourage you. Again, *any* kind of growth will involve more complexity. In some ways, franchising is good because it forces you to get your business organized and properly accounted for.

How to Get Started

I hate to say it, but your first step is to hire a franchise attorney. Franchising is a legal process and requires a good attorney to steer you through it. The second step is to hire an accounting firm to audit your books. The franchiser must have audited statements. Although your professionals will be valuable members of your team, you must make the final decisions on legal and financial matters. Read up on the subjects, and don't just delegate everything to your attorney and your accountant.

If you have a prototype of your business (a successful store or office), then the idea is to outline the essence of what makes it successful and use that information to define your franchise. What exactly are you selling? Are you selling a brand, a proven method of doing business, a service, goods, or some other amenity? If your business involves a physical environment, you will want the store to look a certain way, and you will want to ensure that the product, the marketing methods, the service quality, the hours of operation, and everything else that makes you successful are consistently executed. Your attorney will help you write all this into a contract.

You will also need a disclosure document that is filed with

the Federal Trade Commission and that is given to all prospective franchisees at least ten days before you are allowed to enter into an agreement with them. The disclosure document will detail the terms of the franchise and the background of key business executives, along with the latest financial statements. You must keep careful records of whom you give this document to, and when, so that an unhappy franchisee can't claim later on that he was misled.

Let's put contracts and legal considerations aside. The heart of the matter in franchising is people. Franchisees are people, and they will make your business work if you choose the right ones. Make sure that your vision, whatever it may be, is shared by your franchisees. Are you looking to grow quickly? Is quality the most important thing to you? Customer service? Marketing and publicity? Whatever your hot button is, make sure your franchisees get turned on by the same thing. When I sold franchises, the majority of my franchisees turned out to be former customers—women who had been through the pregnancy experience and understood the market and the void that existed. They were like crusaders who really put their hearts and souls into the Mothers Work franchise. Many of them had been executives who wanted a change of pace after their first baby was born, and a number of them were partnerships of two or three women who shared the workload of the franchise.

Finding your franchisees can be a challenge. Obviously you will advertise in trade publications and small business media. But you should also get creative. We used to append a tag line to all of our mail-order ads that said "Inquire about opening a franchise in your area." We used to get hundreds of responses.

That worked so well that we added that line to our catalog on the back cover. If you're already spending marketing dollars, you might as well make them do double duty for you.

Contract Terms

Exclusive territories. If your franchisee goes to all the work and expense of building a business, he probably won't want you selling another franchise just down the street to compete with him. That is why most franchises, but not all, have exclusive territories within which only they can operate your franchise. This is a good issue to negotiate strongly. The smaller the territory, the more flexibility you will have. Not that you necessarily want to put two franchisees close together. After all, you want your franchisees to be successful. You have the same interest there, but until you start rolling out your concept, you won't really know how close two businesses can be. And once you give that territory away, you will never get it back. I made the mistake of granting a huge territory to my first franchisee—almost three highly populated states. Later I bought part of the territory back and paid a very high price for it. And at the time of granting the franchise, it would have been easy to make it a smaller territory. If you do grant a large territory, at least make provisions in the contract for mandatory multiple locations by the franchisees, on an agreed-upon timetable. That way, if the franchisee doesn't want to keep expanding additional locations, some of the territory can automatically revert to you.

Fees. There are two major types of fees: an initial franchise fee, which gets paid up front upon signing the franchise document, and an ongoing royalty fee, usually a percentage of revenue. The first franchise I sold had no initial franchise fee. I was just happy to have someone get started. After all, I had no prototype store to point to, and no retail track record. So the first franchisee, in a way, was helping me to develop my model store. Later on, as the stores became very successful, I began charging an up-front franchise fee, and as time went on I raised it from around $10,000 to around $30,000. It can really help the cash-flow requirements of growth when you get an initial franchise fee. I also edged up the ongoing royalty fee over time as the brand name and the franchise itself became more proven and valuable. My advice to you is to focus on successful franchises. If you burden them with more fees than they can handle, it won't benefit anyone. Take the long view, and make money by selling more product, not by charging more fees.

Term. Your lawyer will tell you that every contract has to have an ending point. It can't go on forever. Your franchisees will push for a longer term so they can tie up their rights. But you need some point, five years or so, when the contract should come up for renewal so you can have a way of terminating the contract if certain targets are not met. You may have a revenue test or a number of stores, or some other way of evaluating the franchisee. You also might charge a renewal fee to retain the franchise. Again, I wouldn't be greedy about it, but over five years things could change, and the franchise could become much more valuable. It may be good to reassess at that time.

Minimum requirements. This is where you really define your expectations of your franchisees. Whatever you feel really makes your business successful should be outlined. If your concept is a retail store, there should be a minimum number of square feet, possibly an architectural look, hours of operation, even number of salesclerks. Taken to the extreme, McDonald's franchises are 100 percent identical, with specific architectural plans and build-out requirements. Since I had no store model, it was difficult for me to come up with detailed store presentation specifications. I did, however, have an expectation of the amount of merchandise the stores would carry. My franchisees were required to carry a certain percentage of the line of maternity clothes I carried in my catalog. They could buy other lines if they wanted to, but the Mothers Work line had to be "prominently displayed." The then current catalog was actually an exhibit of the franchise contract.

Buyout rights. This is tricky. On the one hand, you want the right to buy out your franchisee at a later date. But trying to lock that into the franchise contract will be a big turnoff to your franchisee. Who wants to work their tail off only to have the franchiser come in and buy their business back cheap? You might try to put some language in the contract that allows you to buy back the contract at the fair market value five or even ten years out, but when you get right down to it, two parties negotiating will reach the fair market value anyway.

And if you force your franchisee to sell when he doesn't want to, he'll probably sue you. Wouldn't you? So although in principle I like the idea of a buyout right, and believe me I wish I had had one, I'm just not sure it is a practical idea. In my case, I ended up buying every single franchise back, and each one was separately negotiated. Some involved lawsuits. It was a long and difficult process. But it can be done!

Life After Franchising

Now you have partners. Treat them like that. Talk to them often, and listen to what they say. They're on the front line, and they can offer valuable information. Getting them all together for a franchise meeting once or twice a year is important. If you don't do it, then they will on their own, and you'll be left out. It can be a little overwhelming when they all get in one room and start complaining (expect that). But airing out grievances is very important. And if you sort out everything that is said, you will learn important ways to improve your business.

It's very important to operate a few company-owned locations yourself. That way you will be tuned into reality and you will know what's really happening. One thing to remember is that you, as the franchiser, are the only one who truly has the big picture about your business. I remember getting into an argument with one of my franchisees about why a particular rule was good for all the franchisees, even if she didn't agree with it. "I don't care about the big picture!" she screamed at me. "I only care about my business!" I guess I really couldn't blame her for feeling that way, but it didn't change the fact that I *did* have to look at the big picture. Your franchise is not a democracy; it is more like a benign dictatorship. It is up to you to decide what is best for the overall health of the franchise. Just remember to listen and be open-minded. And operating a few locations yourself will only help the process.

In summary, franchising your business will allow you to grow quickly with the help of money and talent from other motivated entrepreneurs. But the price is a dilution of your future profit and control, and added complexity. If you and your franchisees share the same vision of the future, and you are fair and open-minded in the way you work together, then franchising can be an excellent choice for growth.

Chapter Six Checklist

▾ Franchising can be a way to grow a business quickly without a lot of capital.

▾ The disadvantage is that franchisees don't work for you—they work for themselves. They may have their own ideas about marketing or running the business.

▾ Start by hiring a franchise attorney, then hire an accounting firm to audit your books.

▾ Create a prototype, culling the essence of what makes it successful, and the ways you want to ensure that the product, marketing, service, and everything else essential are consistently executed.

▾ The real key to franchises is people. Make sure your franchisees share your vision and commitment.

▾ Iron out key terms carefully, such as territory, franchising fees, terms.

▾ Define your expectations of your franchises—whatever you feel makes your business successful.

▾ Include a buyout clause, if possible.

▾ Communicate with your new "partners." Allow them to air grievances.

▾ The cost of franchising is a lessening of your future profit and control, but if your franchisees share the same vision, it can be an excellent way to grow.

chapter seven

Growing Pains

There is nothing more thrilling than being at the helm of a growing business. City by city, we added franchises at lightning speed. San Francisco was run by another eclectic trio of women. An investment banker, a nurse, a housewife. Chicago was bought by a consumer package goods executive. The Denver area was picked up by a grandmother coming out of retirement after her daughter had a baby and she became familiar with Mothers Work. Hartford was run by a man in the pharmaceutical industry whose wife had just had a baby. Atlanta was a husband/wife team. What a group. So much energy. So much excitement, and belief in the future. Each one had a new perspective and new initiatives. We converted Jack Hornsby from a distributor to a franchise at no charge, and his wife opened a Mothers Work store across the street from Hornsby Custom Clothes in Houston.

Things were looking up. We decided we had enough

money to hire a contractor to finish our apartment renovation and we finally got out of the dust. Isaac and Josh started nursery school and I was finally recovered from my surgery. For the first time in years, I could make it through the day without my back killing me. It seemed like everything went in our favor in 1985.

We were hiring like crazy to keep up with our expanding business. First there was an accountant to keep our books and payables straight. (We gave him a title—"controller.") Then there was Lenny, our first real production manager. One of my sewing contractors who knew we were searching for someone recommended him. Lenny was someone who had made garments for a big label in New York. Someone who *knew* what a marker was. He was a little guy in his late fifties, with a heavy Brooklyn accent. And he had that savvy that comes from years of experience. "We are all animals of the trade," he used to say. He was always insinuating things, making you feel that he knew more about apparel than you ever would, so please don't even question me.

The first thing Lenny did was set up a big cutting table in our warehouse and hire a few cutters. This opened up a whole world of contractors who only did sewing, not cutting. It also meant we could start having the fabric delivered right to our own warehouse, and not continually worry about fabric shrinkage. The more control we had over these stages of production, the greater profits and savings we could realize.

Our warehouse was filling up with all the garments Lenny produced. It was only a matter of time before we would have to move to a larger space. Serendipity intervened. Out of the blue one day our landlord called to tell us our warehouse building was being condemned and we had three months to move out. The city was getting ready to tear down an entire four city blocks to make room for the new Pennsylvania Convention Center. They called it eminent domain. I was outraged. I couldn't even believe they could just take our building. This was America, not Russia. What about free enterprise and personal rights and due process? We just moved *into* this warehouse. I would move when *I* was good and ready. Now I understood why there were so many vacancies in the immediate area, and why it was so easy to get a short-term lease. When I called my landlord, he was sympathetic but totally useless.

My next call was to City Hall.

"I want to speak to the mayor." That got me nowhere. After being transferred all around the office I finally ended up with the assistant to the person in charge of relocation for the convention center.

"Someone will be getting in touch with you," she said. How unsatisfying.

One week later we had a meeting with the Office of Relocation for the Convention Center. We learned that as a displaced business we had the right to receive a relocation package, including an outright grant of money to move and relocate as well as a low-interest loan from the Philadelphia Industrial Development Corporation to encourage us to keep our business in the city. The grant was for $25,000. The loan was for $50,000. Now I understood my landlord's lackadaisical attitude. If I was being offered such a rich package, and I was just a tenant, as the owner of the building he probably made out like a bandit.

"That's not enough," I said. "We just put up a new cutting table which we have to disassemble and totally reassemble."

Dan piled on. "This is ridiculous. Maybe we'll move across the river to New Jersey."

"I think I can get you $50,000 on the grant. Would that help?" The relocation administrator was clearly holding back. Who knew how high he could really go?

"Do you realize how much it will cost to fit out another space?" I frowned, showing my displeasure. "Can't you increase the grant?"

Silence.

"I'll give you a $50,000 grant and $75,000 for the loan, and that's my final offer."

"We'll take it," Dan and I both said in unison. Were we too anxious?

"Are you sure that's going to cover us?" I said to Dan, trying to appear unsure. It didn't matter. The guy had already moved on, writing things in his folder.

We wrapped up the meeting and walked out the door. We turned the corner and grinned at each other. "Maybe they'd like to condemn our house too," I said.

So now we were moving again. The Office of Relocation helped us find a new warehouse space a few blocks away, and Lenny took control of moving us "professionally." Gone were the days of a thousand car trips. We hired Vanessa, a recent college graduate, full of energy and smart as a whip, to help us in marketing and franchisee management. We hired Gerta, a real designer, to increase and improve the line. And we had a dozen or so people just filling orders and shipping them out. Our payroll was skyrocketing.

It was looking like this business had a future. Every time we opened a franchised store in a new city we would have another success. There was just nowhere else to buy career maternity clothes. And all of a sudden, yuppies were having babies like crazy. Women in their thirties who had waited until their careers were established before having children. This was a revolution. And Mothers Work was supplying the uniforms. At the rate we were going our sales would be well over $1 million that year. And we were just skimming the surface of this market. We needed to sew up the rest of the market before someone else discovered it. We needed more stores and we needed money to open them.

In the world of getting money, otherwise known as raising capital for your business expansion, there are two sources: debt and equity. Debt you pay back with interest. Equity—which means selling shares of your company—you marry and share the future with, for better or for worse. Most entrepreneurs don't fully think this through. They just know they need money and they take what they can get. But there is a world of difference between the two, and you live with that decision for a very long time. Our history with trying to borrow money was not good, so we turned to the equity side of the equation. Coming from the world of high tech, Dan had a Rolodex full of venture capital contacts. While he started working his files, I started writing a business plan.

I wrestled with that first business plan. How can you possibly forecast your financials five years into the future when you're living hand to mouth, trying to make a payroll every week? Everything was a guess. How big was the market for career maternity clothes? I knew that would be the first question a venture capitalist would ask. But there were no statistics I could find on plain old maternity, let alone a subsection of the market. What about our prior experience in related businesses? Venture capitalists love to invest in someone who is starting a company exactly like the one he just left. My construction engineering experience was useless here. I hauled out all of the old press clippings I could find and tried to validate our idea (thank God my mother had saved them all) and I cobbled together a business plan of sorts, including an elaborate spreadsheet of financial forecasts using Lotus 1-2-3 software. I was up until midnight every night cranking that thing out. It showed that our business would be $10 million in revenue in five years. (At the time, this seemed like a pipe dream. But the truth is we even exceeded that plan. Seven years later, the year before we went public, our business actually did $19 million in sales.)

As soon as I finished the plan we sent it out to Dan's list and then we started a phone follow-up campaign. I would call the reception cool. We got a few very small nibbles and had a couple of short meetings with some junior analysts on staff. We even made a trip to New York to see someone Dan knew well from his computer days. They just didn't love it.

"The market is too small. We only invest in companies where the market is $1 billion or more."

"We only invest in technology companies."

"You don't meet the criteria of our investment portfolio."

And the ever popular:

"If this was such a good idea, someone would already have done it."

We did get the attention of an investor in Connecticut who took the time to come see us in Philadelphia. After a lot of negotiating back and forth he sent us a proposal which was sort of a hybrid investment. We had three years to pay him back *double* his investment of $400,000. And on top of that he would get equity worth half of our company. Did he think we were totally stupid and naive? Did he think we were *that* desperate? We ripped it up and threw it in the trash. I was feeling very underappreciated. Couldn't these people see an opportunity when it was staring them in the face?

"Maybe we have to be a little further along in our development before we can get an investor," Dan said. "Maybe we have to open one of our own stores. Company-owned, not a franchise. So we can demonstrate the potential."

The problem was we had sold all the best territories. New York, Los Angeles, Chicago. All of the big-volume cities belonged to franchisees who had exclusive territories. And the bigger the city, the bigger the store's revenue. For example, Meryl was going gangbusters in New York. It looked like she would sell $500,000 worth of maternity clothes that year out of her one tiny store up on the fifth floor. But since she was selling other lines besides Mothers Work, only about 60 percent, or $300,000, of that revenue was from my product. And since I was selling it to her at roughly 50 percent of the retail price, my revenue was just $150,000. And the gross margin was still not great. We simply had to find a way to have our own retail stores in some big cities. We decided on Boston.

We knew Boston because we had lived there when we were first married. Dan went up to find a location and to recruit a manager. "Store no. 1," as it is still known today, is on the back mezzanine level of an office building in downtown Boston. On Saturdays when the office building is closed, our customers have to sign in at the guard station, wind their way around to the back of the building, find the stairs to the mezzanine level, and ring the buzzer to get into our store. Our philosophy back then was to get a convenient shopping location (we were one block away from Filene's, Jordan Marsh, and all the other big retailers), but in an upstairs or back of the building destination space to cut down on rent. Since career maternity clothes were such a splinter market, we thought that we couldn't afford to pay for space in the big malls, or the first floor on great shopping streets. But we figured that our customers would go the extra mile to seek out our store, since we had a unique product and they had a pressing need.

I took Vanessa to New York to all the maternity showrooms so we could buy some casual maternity clothes to round out the assortment in our store. She was going to be the store buyer after I showed her the ropes. Betty Bailey was getting much more friendly to me, since my franchises were giving her a lot of business. She sent me a coffee cup from Tiffany's at Christmastime. And when I took Vanessa to her showroom the first time, she greeted me at the door like I was her best friend. She had a little tray of fruit and crumpets all laid out, waiting for us. And the funniest thing was when her secretary tried to interrupt us with a call from one of the department stores, and she got this irritated tone of voice. "Take a message, Marianne. Can't you see I'm busy?" I couldn't help but think back to that first time when I visited her showroom and she kicked me out the minute Saks called her. I know it was small-minded of me, but I really enjoyed seeing her suck up to me.

We set up our Boston store in our computer like another mail-order customer account, just as we had done for the franchises. The idea was that we would ship the store an initial stock level of one of each size of each garment. The store manager would keep track of whatever sold in a day and call in an order to replace those items. We would include that order in the day's shipments from the warehouse along with all the mail orders and franchisee orders so that the store would always have a complete selection of our line, except for the one or two prior days' particular sales. This way the manager would know which items to expect on any given day. It was a simple inventory control system which we have stayed with and enhanced over the years. Automatic replenishment driven by customer sales. We don't try to guess which styles will be the most popular and stock larger amounts of those items in the store. Instead, we let the customer lead, and we replenish as often as necessary to keep up with popular styles. Of course, since we make our own product, we can keep the warehouse stocked to fill on demand by remanufacturing as often as necessary. We don't have to depend on another manufacturer's "cutting ticket."

It took about $50,000 to open the Boston store, including all of the fixtures and improvements to the space, and the extra inventory we bought. Every expansion requires capital and it's always on the front end. We were doing well enough to be able to finance this first store, but future stores were definitely going to require the help of an investor. We were all excited about our first official store opening. Lenny declared that he had to be there to see the first customer sale. Vanessa wanted to go too. I wanted everyone to be there for the esprit de corps of the whole thing. But I didn't want to spend a fortune on plane tickets. We decided on People Express, which was the struggling mass-market airline that operated out of Newark. For $37 each, round-trip, we could all go. About ten of us climbed into the big blue van Saturday morning at five and drove up to Newark to get the nine o'clock flight to Boston. The People Express terminal was a zoo. People were lying all over the floor because there weren't enough seats. The plane ride itself was pandemonium. Perfect for a crazy group like us.

It wasn't the biggest store opening we had ever had, but it was definitely the most significant. We probably held down the sales on that day because we attacked every customer who came through the door, we were so overanxious. Finally we were retailers! We could control our own stores and our own destiny. We dragged ourselves home late that night, a tired but happy group.

Over the next few months we nursed our new store along. We hired Miriam to be our retail store director, which made Vanessa a little huffy, but Miriam had a lot more experience actually managing maternity stores. A feisty little gray-haired lady, Miriam looked like someone's grandmother, but she had a ton of energy. She had been the manager of Page Boy Maternity store in the huge regional mall, the Court at King of Prussia. Page Boy was a thirty-store chain of expensive fashion maternity clothes, all located in high-end malls around the country. It was started by two sisters in the 1950s and was based in Dallas. Miriam knew how to run a promotion around Mother's Day and how to manage store presentation, like making the displays look put together and color-coordinated. She was experienced in maintaining the various sale signs and making the front windows look great. And she knew when to take markdowns and how much to discount. She used to go around talking about "my store this and my store that," which drove Vanessa crazy. "They don't belong to *her,*" she'd fume.

It was the first time I had to manage two professionals and the interaction between them. Vanessa, just out of college and trying to make her mark, and Miriam, a grandmother, full of energy, with a ton of experience. Both smart in their own way. They sat across the room from each other, face-to-face, at their desks, which were old hollow-core doors, minus the knobs, on sawhorses and used file cabinets. At first they sniped at each other, which was not terribly productive for the business. Each one wanted to show she was more valuable than the other. But eventually I was able to clearly define each job, with a minimum amount of overlapping responsibility, and they had less cause for arguing. For example, Vanessa had been responsible for the advertising before Miriam came along. But Miriam wanted to place the local advertising that supported "her" stores. She felt that she needed to control various promotions and sales that ran in the stores, and tie them into the advertising. They were always stepping on each other's toes, and actually it was my fault as a manager because I hadn't delineated each one's area of responsibility in a clear way. The problem was solved when I separated the advertising into two areas: local and national. Vanessa did the national ads, and Miriam did the local ones around the stores. Over time, as I worked through their conflicts, and kept focusing them back on doing their jobs well, instead of positioning themselves against each other, they started to get along better.

We were ready to open our next store. We *had* to get some money. The Old Girls Network came through for me. One of Dan's friends from business school was married to a woman banker in New York who had just had a baby and had outfitted herself in Mothers Work suits the entire time. Mary understood the market and the void that existed in career maternity clothes. She also had the business expertise to see that Mothers Work was a viable business for a bank to lend money to. And finally, being a banker herself, she was in a position to help me because she had connections.

We had dinner with Mary and Jim when they were in town one evening. Mary spent the whole evening talking about maternity clothes. She swore she would find us some money to open our next store. Mary's bank was in upstate New York, and she felt that we would be better off with a local Philadelphia-based bank. So she promised that when she got home she would make some calls and see whom she could refer us to. A bank was much more likely to lend us money on Mary's recommendation than if I just called up out of the blue and asked to speak to a loan officer. Mary went to the top, talking to the president of the bank. With just one phone call she accomplished what I heretofore could not.

Mary came through for us. On her strong recommendation, a small Philadelphia bank *called us*. What a switch. We had a meeting and gave it our all. My God, we pitched hard. And now we had a prototype store that was doing well. We walked away with a bank loan for $150,000 to open two more stores. Was it our brilliant negotiating that finally broke through? Our own retail outlet? Or was it the relationship with Mary? I guess a little of each. Another one of those right-place, right-time situations.

At the time, I didn't realize the enormous significance of getting a bank loan. Dan always said it was like getting a girlfriend. It was hard to land the first one, but once you had, it was easy to get another because you were now deemed desirable. Likewise, now we were a "funded" company. A major financial institution had analyzed our company and endorsed it with cash. Suddenly we were on a whole different level. Every future investment emanated from this one. We were plugged into the investment community, whatever that meant.

It didn't take more than two months to spend that money. Dallas was our second store, Cleveland the third. These two stores were not as successful as Boston, but then again neither were those cities' markets. And because our rent was so small, using our secondary-location strategy, the stores were still very profitable. We were still opening franchises too. Harrisburg and San Diego opened during this time. The Mothers Work juggernaut was rolling forward.

More opportunity. We needed more money. Always more money. Sometimes I think the history of any company is in the story of how it raised money. This time we were going to need equity. Our borrowing capacity was tapped out. Bankers have two key financials ratios they use to analyze the capacity for additional borrowing. One is the coverage ratio, which is more or less your monthly earnings divided by your monthly loan repayment amount, to make sure you can afford the loan payments. The other is the total amount of your debt divided by the total amount of your equity, where equity is all the sources of capital besides debt that have been put into the business over time, including the earnings that have accumulated. The debt to equity ratio ensures that if you go bankrupt, there is enough there for the bank to be repaid in full. Both ratios showed that we had as much bank debt as we could handle. It was clear that we needed more equity.

But now we had connections. Now we were plugged in. Our banker arranged a meeting with an attorney who worked for a lot of venture capitalists. The attorney arranged a meeting with a private investor. At the same time, our accountants introduced us to some other private investors. I hauled out the old business plan and started rewriting it. Everything was different now. We were a funded company. I won't say it was anything approaching easy, but at least people were willing to talk to us now.

Our first meeting was with two successful businessmen, both in their sixties, who had formed an investment club with five or six of their successful business friends. They invested in start-ups, relying on all of the combined experience they had in different industries. Two captains of industry climbing up the steep creaky stairway of our crappy walk-up. One of them had a bad knee. They were huffing and puffing when they got up there. Not an auspicious beginning.

One was in the computer chip business. The other was the vice-chairman of the largest department store chain in Philadelphia. He really knew something about retailing.

"So tell me, Rebecca," the retailing expert asked, still panting after climbing those stairs, "how do you close out your merchandise at the end of the season? Do you take a lot of markdowns?"

I told him that we just send it back to the warehouse and then sell it the next year. I explained that the clothes are *classics,* they never go out of style, so I never mark them down.

"Well, doesn't your inventory get a little heavy? What kind of turn do you have?"

I had a vague idea that turn had something to do with how fast your merchandise sold, versus how much was just sitting around collecting dust. And now that he mentioned it, our inventory was getting pretty large, but our sales were growing too. We *needed* more inventory. This whole language was new to me. I really had no idea what the size of our turn was. I just made clothes that customers wanted to buy.

"Our inventory is efficient," I said, sort of faking it as I went along. "Our warehouse services our stores, our franchises, *and* our mail order. That's why our turn is constantly improving." That seemed to satisfy him. The phone rang. I leaped up and grabbed it, forcing Dan to answer the next hard question. It was St. Peter's School. The headmistress. I turned my back to the group so they couldn't hear me.

"Mrs. Matthias, I'm concerned about Josh. Can you come in to see us sometime this week?" Josh had just started three-year nursery school at St. Peter's.

"Oh yes, I can set up a meeting with you this week. Exactly what will we be discussing?" I was trying to make it sound like a business call.

"Is something happening at home, Mrs. Matthias? Josh's teacher is noticing a behavioral pattern that is disturbing. He only draws with black crayons."

Black crayons? She was calling me about black crayons? Here I was trying to close a venture capital deal and she wants to talk about black crayons? Had they ever offered him a red crayon? I wanted to ask her that, but I didn't think it would further my cause with my potential investors. They were staring at me now.

"Yes, well, I'd like to talk to you about that color choice. I'll have to check my calendar and call you back with a time for that meeting. Thanks a lot. Bye now."

I tried, but I could no longer focus on the meeting. All of a sudden, venture capital seemed relatively unimportant. Was I destroying my child's well-being in some way? He seemed like such a happy kid. I knew the headmistress had a tacit disapproval for working mothers. Was she just blowing something out of proportion?

I brooded about Josh for the next few days until our meeting with the headmistress. In the meantime, we learned not only that the first two venture capitalists were interested in making an investment but that we had another interested investor. The attorney from our bank wanted to make the introduction, but as it turned out, this new lead had already made some other investments jointly with our venture capitalists. The fact that they were interested in Mothers Work probably made us seem like a good investment. Going on Dan's girlfriend theory, we were hot.

We had a second meeting with our original venture capitalists and this new interest. He was an easygoing type. I couldn't believe how young he was to be managing so much money. He breezed into our meeting thirty minutes late and then pulled out a bag of M&M's and started eating them.

"Hope you don't mind if I have a snack," he said, grinning. "I didn't have time for lunch. Nice company you have here. Career maternity. I know a lot of women who could use your product."

He seemed so casual about it. Of course I learned later, after getting to know him, that he had thoroughly researched our company before even stepping into the meeting. But once again, the fact that he was in the age group of people who personally experienced the need for the product made him understand the market and the compelling customer demand. He seemed more interested in getting to know us as people, and we hit it off with him right from the start.

When the meeting was adjourned, Dan and I realized that we were about to actually get a cash injection of $500,000 into our growing business. This would be the start of something really big. We started to calculate how many stores we could open with that money. Suddenly our company was in the big leagues. We had investors. We had a bank. We were going to grow like crazy. We had gotten other people to believe in our idea, and they were going to back us financially. I thought back to that first reply envelope I had received. That first order for $247. I couldn't believe how far I had come. Yet, I was just entering a new world of venture capital and high finance, board meetings and annual reports. It seemed like every time I reached a level of achievement, a new door opened with new challenges and new aspirations. Once again, I was a novice with a lot to learn.

The headmistress at St. Peter's was an imperious type who ruled the school. Isaac used to call her "the lady who owns the school." As Dan and I sat in her office, later that week, she grilled us about our homelife and Josh's malaise.

"Maybe he's upset because I had to be in Dallas last week." I didn't want to admit too much, but I was trying to offer up some explanation. *Mea culpa, mea culpa, I know I'm a bad mother.*

"Mrs. Matthias, a child is like a little flower. He needs sunshine and water every day. Do you think Josh is getting enough sunshine?"

Oh my God, I could see where this was leading. I was going to be portrayed as the cold north wind. Who the hell did she think she was to judge me like that? Josh had more sunshine than any kid I knew. He had *two* sets of parents who loved him. I went on the offensive.

"What exactly is Josh doing that makes you think he has a problem? I mean besides drawing with black crayons."

This made her stop for a minute. Then she reverted to psychobabble.

"The choice of black in a child's color palette can indicate a much deeper behavioral deviation. It's our duty to surface these dysfunctional patterns so they can be dealt with."

I beg your pardon? I was starting to understand where this problem was coming from. And it wasn't me.

We concluded our meeting and walked home, shaking our heads. That night we sat on the couch with our three-year-old and talked about school. We talked about art. And we talked about black crayons. And we uncovered the real problem. They didn't give Josh any pencils to draw with and black crayons were the closest thing he could find. I was always going around sketching in pencil, and he was imitating me and the way I drew, just as a little duckling follows his mother into a pond for its first experience of the water. Maybe I wasn't such a terrible mother.

Mothers Work was heading into its fifth year in business. They say that if a company can make it through five years, the odds of long-term survival escalate. Except that for us, every year seemed like we were starting a completely new business as we developed and grew. Did that mean we had to constantly start the clock over? We were about to mark our first year as a retailer. The year before that we were a franchiser, and the year before that we were a mail-order company. The fifth year would prove to be one of the most, let's just say, interesting. You think everything is sailing along, and then you hit a squall. Everyone does. The real question is how do you react? How do you handle adversity? Are you able to get going when the going gets rough? The sailboat was about to tip over and it was all I could do to stay out of the drink.

How to Raise Money and Keep the Cash Flowing

▼ ▼ ▼

If you plan to grow your business, you will play the money-raising game. It may seem counterintuitive, but the more successful your company is, the more money you will have to raise. Of course you always have the option for slow growth, using your retained earnings, and there is certainly a lot to recommend this choice: no one to interfere with your operations, no one to account to, and no one to share the future rewards. There are definitely some people who should never invite anyone else into their business, because they just aren't willing to give up any control. But sometimes a smaller percentage of a larger pie can yield more pie for you. And growing the pie takes dough. As usual, there is no right or wrong answer here. It's all up to you!

The first step in any money-raising initiative is writing a business plan. You must communicate the essence of your business, including your vision of the future, to anyone who would be interested in giving you money. The next step is to decide whether you are looking for debt or equity or a combination of both. In all probability, debt will come from a bank, but it could also come from your mother or a friend, or a private investor. Debt will be paid back with interest on a defined schedule. If you are borrowing money from a relative or a friend, it is *crucial* to be specific about whether it is debt or equity. I have seen relationships destroyed when this is not spelled out. If things go sour, will you pay back the investment (debt)? Or will your partner share the pain and lose her investment along with you (equity)? Equity will give you a partner in your business. When you succeed, your partner will share the wealth proportionately. That original $10,000 investment, made at a time when you were desperate, and which bought 30 percent of your company, could turn into millions of dollars, or it could be totally lost.

How to Write a Business Plan

Your business plan will have a written section and a financial one. There is no specific form that you must follow, but there are certain key areas you should cover. Just like the length of a great speech—no longer than twenty minutes—a great business plan should never be too long. Twenty pages is not a bad length. Start off with a one- or two-page summary of your business that is compelling and easy to grasp. This may be the *only* section that most people read. You want to get across to your potential investor why your business has a great future, what your unique advantage is, and why you are better than the competition. Highlight the key numbers, whether they are sales, sales growth, profitability, sales per square foot, or cash-flow generation. Anything truly impressive that you can think of belongs in the summary section.

Obviously the specific nature of your business will dictate exactly what the written part of your business plan should cover, but here are a few sections that almost every plan should have.

The market. How big is the total market for your product? If you can't give specific numbers, then approximate. You must quantify it in some way. This was very difficult for me because there were no government numbers on the maternity apparel market. So I obtained information on total number of births and combined that with demographic numbers and statistics on workingwomen to try to approximate the size of the total maternity market and the career maternity market. The funny thing is that, later on, an article regarding maternity clothes in a large metropolitan newspaper reported that the total maternity market was $500 million in size. Their source? Me. They took my back-of-the-envelope calculations and repeated them as if they were gospel.

The competition. Everyone has competition. I used to take the position with career maternity clothes that I had none. But looking back, I think that hurt my case. Obviously these women were buying clothes *somewhere.* It's expected that you have competition. The important thing is to know who they are and to have a plan to beat them.

Strategy. This is the guts of your business plan. How will you achieve your goals? Franchise? Acquire? Dominate your market or carve out a small niche within it? One of the key aspects of my business plan was to be vertically integrated. That simply means we manufacture the product that we retail. This gave me control over my product, and better gross margin. This section is your chance to tell your story and explain what your plan is.

Product. Pretty straightforward. What it is and why it is fabulous.

Financials. Most people get hives about this section of their business plan. I know I did. The history part is easy. Give income statements and balance sheets as far back as you have them, although not beyond five years. The future is more problematic. You need to show a financial forecast for the next year, month by month, and then at least two and preferably five years out, in full years. There are tons of software packages that you can use to construct your financial model. The key is to imagine the future. You have to see your company two or five years from now and describe it in financial terms. How many more people will you hire? How many widgets could you sell if you had the money to put into the inventory? Look at it from the bottom up, adding up all the little pieces, all the accounts you have now and how many more you could have. Then look at it top down. If you owned 30 percent of the market, how much revenue would that be? Now what kind of overhead do you need to support it? No one is better prepared to make those judgments than you. We're talking about the vision thing. You have to have it to lead your company into the future and convince a lender or an investor to go there with you.

Debt—Getting Your First Bank Loan

Now that you have your business plan, you have a weapon in the money wars. You have something to show to a lender. Banks are looking for one thing. They want to get paid back. With interest. This may be obvious to some people, but others may mistakenly think that banks want to help women and minorities, or that they want to build the local economy, or that they want to get in on the ground floor of a growth company. Those things are far down on the list.

Most banks take a belt-and-suspenders approach to small business lending because so many small businesses fail and don't pay their loans back. Not only will your lender want to see a viable business plan that she believes can support the loan payments, she will also want to get her hands on some type of asset that she can grab if everything else fails. That can be the inventory in the company (valued at a fraction of its cost), or it can be your house or your 401(K) account. Banks hate risk. They want to see that you've invested all of your personal savings into the business so that you are *really* committed to making this thing work. If you have money you haven't put into the business, or assets, like your house, that you haven't pledged as collateral, they will think that you're holding back and not risking it all. And furthermore, they want as much capital in the business as possible to increase the chances of its survival. They will definitely want to see several years of a track record. Don't even think of asking a bank to fund a brand-new start-up with no history. They're not in that business.

Banks don't necessarily have to see huge growth plans in your business. In fact, they prefer steady, rock-solid cash flow. So when you give your bank a forecast, don't overextend yourself. They'll just use it against you by building covenants into your loan that are tied to that performance. Then, if you fall short, nasty penalties can kick in. Often they take first claim on more of your assets, or they reduce the size of your loan. Remember, banks don't make loans based on your pie-in-the-sky forecast. They're looking to solid historical performance, and they will structure their loan to protect *their* investment, not yours.

The nice thing about banks is that they are easy to find. They're all right there in the yellow pages, and you can methodically go down the list, sending out your business plan and calling the small business officer of every bank. Just because one bank says no, don't despair. Keep trying. They all have different appetites for various industries and business types. Sometimes timing can be everything, depending on whether they are trying to increase their portfolios or not. And sometimes chemistry can make the difference. Bankers, contrary to popular belief, are only human.

How to Get Your First Equity Investor

I'm not talking about your parents. I assume you've already tapped them. I'm talking about a professional investor who invests her own or a pool of other people's money with an eye toward making a killing down the road. In some ways, getting an equity investor is the true test of the viability of your business. Evaluating growth businesses is the way these guys make their living. They look at hundreds of business plans every *week.* And they're brutal to deal with. They'll poke and prod your business from every angle, looking for the flaws. They'll make you feel like two cents, and then they'll send you a form letter telling you that your business doesn't fit into their investment criteria at the present time. Believe me, this activity is not for the thin-skinned. Persistence is key.

Sometimes it's just a matter of finding the right match. Some funds only invest in high tech. Others only deal with later-stage companies. Some have minimum dollar investment criteria. And there is no really good way of sorting it all out. This industry is not listed in the yellow pages. You have to start some sort of trail, and keep pursuing leads—i.e., networking. Your lawyer and your accountant are the logical first step. In larger cities there will be some sort of venture capital organization that can provide a listing and may have venture fairs or other opportunities to present your business plan.

The private investors who invest their own money ad hoc are the hardest to find, but are my favorite source. These people are usually businesspeople who earned and invest their own money. They know what it means to meet a payroll, and they can really give you some operating advice instead of just looking at financials. You can be proactive and place an ad in your local business news, "Great emerging small business looking for investing angel."

You can't blame equity investors for being tough on potential investments. After all, they stand to lose all of their money if you don't make it. If you do attract an investor, just remember you are giving up part of your future rewards. If the deal isn't good enough, if you're giving up too big of a piece for too little money, you can *just say no.* If your back is against the wall, this is not the time to raise money anyway. I know this is easy to say, and hard to live by, but the truth is no one will invest in a money-losing business. Put yourself in the investor's shoes. If you had a lot of hard-earned money and you were looking for an opportunity to invest in, would you run out and invest in a company that was so desperate to get funds it would go bankrupt unless it got money right away? Of course not. If you are desperate, they will know. *You can only raise money when you don't need it.* So help me this is true. I always advise small business owners to manage their way through a cash crisis, and when they get to the other side, then go out and raise money. String out your suppliers, borrow more from your mother, hunker down, fire a few people if you must, but get by.

Whether you raise money through debt or equity, you are taking in a partner who has an interest in the success of your business, and who will want some say in how you operate it. Just like choosing a franchisee, when you choose an investor, make sure you can get along with your new partner. The people part of the equation is an important one. Any venture capitalist will tell you that they invest in people, not businesses. Be sure you share the same vision of the future and that your styles are compatible. Getting a divorce can be a messy and time-consuming disaster. Treat your investor like the partner that she is, and you will have a happy marriage.

Chapter Seven Checklist

▾ The first step in raising money is writing a business plan.

▾ The next step is to decide whether you want to obtain funding through a loan (usually from a bank or an investor) or from the sale of equity in the company.

▾ In creating a business plan, write a one- or two-page summary of your business that is compelling and easy to grasp.

▾ Explain how big the total market is for your product.

▾ Define your competition—and outline your strategy to compete against them, month by month, for two to five years.

▾ On getting your first bank loan, remember banks want to see several years of a track record.

▾ Don't overextend yourself when giving a bank a forecast—and remember, timing can be everything. If one turns you down, go on to the next one.

▾ To find an equity investor, you must network and pursue leads religiously.

chapter eight

Managing Chaos

Funny how quickly the tables can turn. There we were barreling along with money in the bank, growing rapidly, and the next thing I knew we were out of money, out of cities to open franchises, and laying off employees in an attempt to reduce overhead and cover the remaining ones. The result was that Dan and I had to resume doing all of the things that we had hired them to do. "Stretched thin" doesn't even begin to describe how harried and stressed-out we both were during this period of time. Dan was running around to sewing contractors, and I was taking the 7:35 A.M. train to New York to buy clothes for our stores. We put our own meager salaries on hold for six months while we tried to build some cash. How had it happened?

In many ways we were victims of our own success. We grew so fast with the franchisees that when we finally opened our own stores, they were all in secondary markets. They cost just as much to build as the high-volume stores, but they didn't produce as much. We went into Boston with a second, better store location on the main street, but we ended up taking business from store no. 1. We opened in Costa Mesa, California, but the real market was in Los Angeles, which already had a franchise. And all the while, our inventory was growing and sucking up huge amounts of cash.

Meanwhile, we were having a quality control problem with the garments that we were making. We were growing so quickly that we couldn't keep up. So we ended up with all of our work in a few factories, which couldn't really handle the load. The stuff was starting to come out really ratty, and the franchises were starting to complain.

The last straw came when our largest sewing contractor delivered three hundred jumpers with the worst quality imaginable. The top stitching along the front edge of the garment wasn't even straight. It was weaving back and forth. Dan was taking all the plastic off one by one and looking at them. Each one was worse than the last. I was getting a sick feeling in the bottom of my stomach. "How can you possibly expect me to sell these?" I screamed at the contractor. "You have to rework them."

We spent the rest of the day going through all three hundred jumpers and came to the conclusion not only that this contractor had destroyed this lot, but if we allowed him to, he would destroy the other two or three thousand garments that he was working on. I could visualize the piles of cut pieces lying around his shop, waiting to be assembled. We had to get them before they were assembled in the same shoddy fashion as the jumpers. I was thinking about the orders I had that weren't going to get filled. I was wondering how on earth we were going to fix these jumpers and two or three thousand other things. Dan said, "I'm going over to get everything and bring it back." He rounded up a few of our order pickers to help him. Lenny followed them out the door. Dan and his crew got into the big blue van, drove to the sewing shop, and picked up three thousand garments in various stages of completion. Lenny went home. I guess it had become too stressful for him. Who could blame him? It was too stressful for me too. But I had no choice other than to carry on. I couldn't quit.

Dan threw himself into finding new contractors who could deliver with quality. My God, the last thing in the world we could afford to lose was our reputation for great clothes. Really, that was all we had. The competition out there was fierce. Every time you turned around, someone else was getting into the business. Page Boy was increasing its line of career clothes, and they had huge amounts of traffic because of the big malls they were in all over the country. And then there was a new start-up company in Dallas called A Pea in the Pod. I heard they were backed by a big venture capital firm, and they were starting to open stores all over. Their product was high-fashion and expensive. Even though they weren't targeting career per se, they were definitely overlapping my market. Then there were the regional chains, like Recreations, which had twenty or thirty stores in Ohio. And there were three or four "me too" catalogs, like Diane's Designs, along with Career Maternity Collection, which practically photocopied my catalog, it was so similar. Of course Saks and the other department stores were out there too. And I'm not even counting the lower-priced chains like Motherhood, Dan Howard Factory Outlet, and Mothercare.

Although we had a splashy start with the franchises opening strong, the competition was holding us back, and sales gains were getting hard to come by. It seemed like we were hitting a wall. And as usual, we didn't have the financial resources to break through. Actually, some of the franchises were doing better than we were, because many of them had started carrying more and more clothes from other maternity manufacturers. They could make more money selling another line, because they had no restrictions on how much they marked it up. For example, they could buy a cheap dress off someone else's moderate line for, say, $25, and mark it up to $100. They would make $75 on every dress they sold. That would compare to the Mothers Work $100 dress for which they paid $50, and therefore only made $50 when it was sold. You see, they were locked into the 50 percent price markup with us because all of the retail prices were published in the catalog, and by contract they paid 50 percent for all of the clothes. But they had no restrictions on how much they marked up product that they purchased from other manufacturers.

What they were really doing was milking the Mothers Work brand, which stood for high quality, at a fairly high price, by selling cheaper clothes under our logo and making a huge markup. And since we were locked out of their territories, they were limiting our opportunity to sell more of our product in those cities. It was something that we had never anticipated when we were selling franchises, and so we hadn't protected ourselves in the contract. There was really nothing we could do about it. The only contract protection we did have was the requirement that the franchises at all times carried 85 percent of our line, as it was represented in the catalog at any given point in time. Beyond that, they could carry as much or as little else as they wanted to.

So the franchises seemed to be doing fine. *They* didn't have huge overheads to support. *They* didn't need to keep growing to get to a profit level. *They* didn't need to run out and open more stores in their huge territories. Yes, they were entrepreneurial, but their idea of success was much smaller than ours. They were happy at their current level, with no desire to grow any larger and risk what they had already built. Most of them were already making more money than they ever thought they could. And we had spent all our money on two or three new stores and huge amounts of inventory to support them and support the big network of franchised stores. Furthermore, we had let our overhead get ahead of us. We had all kinds of new expenses including accounting and legal bills. We also had more advertising expenditures to fight all the competition, and we had a huge payroll. On top of everything, we had to start paying back our bank loan, with interest. We knew we wouldn't be able to raise any more money. I mean, what would an investor be investing in? Where was the future growth? Where were the historical profits? The only thing we could do was reevaluate and regroup. We had to get our overhead down to what we could support under the current revenue level. Then we'd go from there.

As hard as it was, we knew we had to lay off some of our workforce, including some of the key people. Lenny went first. Then Vanessa and Miriam were chopped off. We had to save money and, sadly, employees are usually the first to go. It was the first time I had to let some go and it was horrible. I hated letting them down. I hated being defeated. But unless we could get control of our cash flow, we'd be out of the game completely. Meanwhile Dan and I both stopped drawing our salaries, which we had only started taking when we got our initial investment. Believe me, that hurt my pride as much as my pocketbook. We hired one new person as sort of an overall assistant at a fraction of what we saved with the layoff.

I'm sorry to say that this was not the last time in the life of my company that I had to face layoffs in order to bring expenses in line. Growth never happens in a straight line, and trying to match the rate of hiring with the rate of sales increase can be impossible. As hard as it is, you have to react and control your expenses. It's the only way to keep your company intact and save the remaining employees. On top of the personal pain of letting valuable employees go, we had to live with the guilt. I often felt like a rat, and the very real infestation of rats in our warehouse was an all-too-real reminder of how decidedly unglamorous our lives were as entrepreneurs.

Once again, Dan and I were scrambling to stay above water. Thank God for my parents, because they pitched in with the kids, the household, and everything else. Dan and I hardly ever took our turns making dinner anymore, and my father was always there to take the kids to nursery school and pick them up too. Dan managed the contractors, and I handled the New York buying trips and the inventory control.

Slowly I knew we'd climb our way back up, looking every day for small opportunities. I still believed that we had the making of a big success if we could just keep it going until we saw our opening. We tried different ways of breaking out in the absence of another investment. We dreamed up alternate means of financing. Creative financing. For example, there was the Group IPO Idea.

The Group IPO Idea went something like this. We may only have a $3-million-dollar company, but the whole Mothers Work group of twenty franchises, if you rolled it up into one big company, has about $15 million of revenue, which is big enough to go public. Let's get all of the franchises to join together with us and we'll all take a share of a new corporation, which will be the amalgamation of the whole chain of franchise and company stores plus mail order. Then we'll all get rich because the sum of the parts will be greater when they are added together. Two plus two will equal five. Obviously no single Mothers Work franchisee would be big enough to have a public offering, but if we throw our fortunes together, we can do it as a group. Dan and I got on the phones one day and started calling all the franchisees to try to sell them on that brilliant idea. Do I need to tell you we got nowhere? These people weren't about to give up a good thing. Furthermore, they didn't trust anyone else to run their business, and they had no intention of banding together with anyone. Each one thought her own business was worth more, was better managed, was far superior to all the other franchises. And they liked being small business owners.

Then there was the Eat Something Bigger Than Your Head Idea. Obscure the problem by acquiring a much larger, related business, and bring in lots of new investment to support the new and the old businesses combined. We had something in mind here too. There was a Philadelphia-based company that had fifty maternity stores in the Pennsylvania/New Jersey region. They also had sixty or seventy large-size stores (nonmaternity). Their prices were way below ours, so it would take us in a whole different direction, but their revenue level was in excess of $30 million, so it would leapfrog us into the big time. What gall we had to approach them. Our little $3-million operation. I guess we had very little to lose, and at a minimum we would see how another maternity company operated.

The owner agreed to see us, so we drove up to her office one morning. She had a real building in an office park with a manicured lawn in front. The receptionist showed us in to her spacious corner office and we stood around waiting for her. I was getting cold feet about the whole idea. We waited and waited. Finally she waltzed in. She was about fifty-five years old, a short, somewhat rotund woman, wearing a pink velour sweat suit and white cowboy boots. "Siddown!" she bellowed at us, motioning to a couple of chairs. I think my jaw was hanging open. This was a woman in charge. She dressed however the hell she felt like, and was totally at ease bossing people around. We followed orders and sat in her blue suede love seat. I was still staring at her, tongue-tied, so Dan jumped in.

"Quite an operation you have here," he said.

"Yeah, I built it up from scratch. It's a tough market out there. But you seem to have found a new way to approach it." She was generous enough to throw an offhanded compliment our way. Looking around the office, I could see one of our catalogs peeking out from a pile of stuff on her desk. This woman didn't miss a thing.

"We've been looking for opportunities to grow," he said. "Ways to combine with other companies in the industry. Maybe a strategic alliance, or a way to share resources, or even a merger." Dan was so diplomatic.

"Maybe we could even acquire your company," I blurted out. Let's get to the point.

The owner looked at us. She smiled. Then she started to laugh. One of those big hearty laughs. "I think it's the other way around. Maybe I should buy you."

She had a point. I found out what I came for and I was ready to go. But Dan talked us politely through another few minutes, and then she had someone show us around the office. Finally we slinked out with our tails between our legs.

Okay, so that didn't work. Back to the salt mines. Back to the business of everyday making clothes and shipping them to our customers. Seeing what sells and designing more things like it. Managing the overhead. Working with the warehouse team to show them how to do their job a little better. Negotiating twenty-five cents a yard off our biggest-selling cotton shirt fabric. Doing the thousand little unglamorous things that would make our business a little better every day.

Then there was the fire. The fire started in the building next to our warehouse. Dan was driving back from a new sewing contractor in New Jersey, over the Ben Franklin Bridge, when he saw big black clouds in the sky, kind of in the garment center area. He knew it before I did. I was inside trying to supervise the end-of-the-day scramble to get all the packages out to the UPS truck by four. We smelled the fire before we saw it. Then we heard the fire sirens. Next thing we knew our building fire alarm was wailing and firemen were going floor to floor evacuating our building. We all trooped down the five floors of stairs. When I got down, Dan was just pulling up in the van. We all stood across the street from our building and watched. Flames were shooting out from the warehouse building next to ours. There was a little alley separating the two buildings, but the fire was trying to jump across the alley and get into ours. The police came and started blocking off the whole street and getting everyone to move away. There was nothing we could do.

Our whole lives were tied up in that crappy warehouse. We must have had $1 million of inventory. What if it all burned down? Sure we had insurance, but what would we get, $500,000? A million? Most of it would go to the bank and our investors anyway. I hadn't killed myself for five years to watch it all go up in smoke. How could we recover all that merchandise? It would take months to remanufacture it. We watched the fire on the evening news while we ate dinner, hoping the firemen would get it under control. I would never complain about paying city taxes again.

At around eight o'clock Dan started getting antsy. "Let's go back over and see what's happening." Back into the van. We parked a few blocks away, knowing the street would still be blocked off. When we got to the warehouse, the firemen were still working, going strong. The police had barricades set up all around the building, and there were all kinds of activity. The burning building was still smoldering, even though there had to be five huge fire hoses spraying from every angle. The windows on the side of our warehouse that faced the burning building were all black and burned out. The firemen were hosing that side of the building down, and I could practically see our clothes getting soaked and sooty. Big black smoke clouds wafted into our building through the broken windows. But the building itself seemed to have been spared from the blaze.

In the confusion, Dan and I were able to sneak through the barricades and walk the five flights up to our floor. All the lights were out because the electric was down. Luckily Dan had brought a flashlight. We passed some firemen on a couple of floors, but I guess they were too preoccupied to notice us. When we got to our floor, we could just make out the extent of the damage. We tried to get over to the windows that were burned out, but they were blocked by the smoke and heat from the still smoldering building across the alley. I could see some of the dresses that were close to the window. *Oh my God, there's style no. 501A. Our best-selling dress. We just received that lot yesterday, and I have orders still to fill.* I started grabbing some of the dresses off the rack and running them to the other side of the building away from the fire. Dan grabbed a whole rack of jackets and slid them away from the window. We worked for five or ten minutes pulling things back from the window before one of the firemen found us.

"What are you doing up here?" he yelled at us. "You can't be here. Everyone has to be out of this building. This is a *fire* zone."

I grabbed one more handful of blouses on our way out. When we got back downstairs, we noticed several men in business suits and coats wandering around. One of them approached us.

"Are you a tenant?" he asked. "Do you need an adjuster?"

Without admitting anything I said, "What's an adjuster?"

"I can help you collect on your insurance," the man answered. "I'll get you more than any other adjuster can." He was thrusting his business card at me.

What was he talking about? Why did we need him? I was already paying my insurance company. Why would I pay him too? By the time we threaded our way through the crowd and left, we had three cards from different insurance adjusters.

We went home and worried the rest of the evening. At least our building hadn't burned to the ground. But there was clearly a lot of damage done to the inventory and the space itself. And naturally we had an insurance policy with a big deductible in order to save money. The first $50,000 of fire damage wasn't even covered. I couldn't believe this was happening.

When we got to the warehouse the next day, the firemen were gone. The electric was still out, so we had to walk up the five floors. Everything was covered in black soot, and there was water on the floor from the fire hoses. We started to sort through the clothes to see what was lost. Fortunately every garment was covered in plastic, so the soot didn't penetrate the clothes. But a number of garments were so close to the windows that the plastic melted right off. And almost everything had a smoky smell to it that was going to make them hard to sell. We decided that we should call one of the adjusters who had given us their cards the night before, just to see what he had to say. He was there in twenty-two minutes.

He walked through the space with us, looking at the damage. He asked to see our insurance policy, which he read as he walked. Then he asked me a couple of questions about how much the garments cost and what they retailed for.

"I think you have a pretty healthy claim here," he said. "Maybe $100,000. Maybe $200,000. I'll take 10 percent of what I get for you."

I was floored. I wouldn't have even thought to ask for that much. I mean, if we sorted out the garments that were truly damaged, not just soot on the plastic, there couldn't be that many that were lost. Dan and I excused ourselves for a minute to talk it over. It was pretty obvious that we had nothing to lose by letting this man represent us. We didn't really want to have to deal with the insurance company anyway. We walked back over to him.

"I'll give you 8 percent," I said.

"Nine and it's a deal." He held out his hand, and we all shook.

We spent the rest of the day cleaning up and getting organized again. The adjuster didn't want us to touch any of the damaged garments until the insurance company could see it all for themselves, so it was actually a week or so until things got anywhere close to normal. When all was said and done, we ended up with a check for $176,433.89. It seemed like our disasters were more lucrative than our successes. Sure we lost a lot of merchandise, but truthfully we were overinventoried anyway.

That year was chaotic. Weird things kept happening. After the fire, the Pittsburgh franchisee gave us the franchise back. It was an unusual franchisee anyway. It was run by one of the Pittsburgh hospitals, which had a large obstetrics department. The president was this very innovative, marketing type of person who opened a pregnancy education center with seminars and classes, and other services for pregnant women. He thought that running a Mothers Work maternity store would round out the service. He really went at it in a professional way too. He hired a top-notch retailing executive to run the store, and they loaded it up with inventory. They spent a lot of money on advertising and distributed the catalog in their new-mom packages. It seemed like a natural. The only thing was, they didn't have a real knack for making a profit. They were so concerned with the service aspect, they forgot that a business has to make money. So all the overhead they loaded onto it couldn't be supported. Rather than stay with it and fix it, they just got tired of it and gave it back to us. Of course we were happy to take it. They *gave* us the inventory. All we had to do was take over the lease on their space.

So now we had one more store. But we needed more. We needed more distribution than the franchises were going to give us. Their growth was increasingly coming from other manufacturers' products. We decided that we were going to have to confront them and see if they were living up to their end of the bargain—whether they were really carrying 85 percent of our line. We decided to audit their stores to check. Physically go into the stores with a list of our styles and count what they had, to see if they met the test. After all, there was no way for us to know any other way. We were relying solely on them. We knew how much they ordered, but we didn't have an itemized record of what they sold, just their total revenue dollars. And because they could carry unlimited amounts of other vendors' merchandise, there was no way to know how much of their sales came from other vendors vs. Mothers Work. It was impossible to calculate how much Mothers Work merchandise they had at any point in time without physically counting it.

I did most of the counting. Our accountants helped in some of the remote cities where they had branches. I flew to some cities. Most of them complied, and those who didn't said they would do better. The Philadelphia store was way under the correct count. I insisted that the situation be corrected if they wanted to stay a franchise, but I think they were making so much more money by marking up other cheaper lines that they really didn't want to. In the end, we decided to terminate our franchise agreement, and they changed the name of their store.

Now we had the opportunity to open a new store in Philadelphia, and we wanted to make it great. Philadelphia was the largest city that we had tackled so far. We wanted to experiment with a new concept: malls. Now, I know what you're thinking. Every person with half a brain knows that malls are where America shops. But up until then we had been scared to death of the huge rents they commanded. And not being crazed consumers ourselves, I guess the whole mall mania had gone by us. I had always lived in urban areas, and I never shopped in malls. But recently the troika from Washington, D.C., had opened a second store in a big regional mall and the results had been staggering. If they could do that much, think what we could do at the Court at King of Prussia, which dominated the entire tristate shopping scene of Pennsylvania, New Jersey, and Delaware. The knowledge we had gained about the huge volume of business that Page Boy Maternity Store did in the same mall emboldened us with our decision. So we took some of the money from the fire and put it toward store no. 7. In the mall. We were about to find our future.

In order to minimize the rent expense, we took a tiny little 642-square-foot space. We figured that we'd replenish the inventory every day anyway, so we didn't need a huge space to hold multiples of each style. We didn't even build a back room. We used every available inch of that space for selling. And we merchandised clothes right up the wall. The sales associates had to use hooks to get things down for the customers. The store did better than we ever expected. We did almost $600,000 in the first year out of that tiny space, and the store was the biggest profit contributor of all seven stores we owned, even with the high rent we were paying. Our eyes were being opened to the idea of customer traffic, and just how important it was, even in a business like maternity where only one out of two hundred people going by the door can use your product. The old saw pertained even to us: location, location, location—the three most important factors in real estate and retailing. We learned it the hard way.

It was becoming clear to us that the path to success lay in mall stores that we owned and operated. The franchises had a different view of life than we did, and what had once seemed like a great idea was now blocking our continued growth. We had sold our birthright and now we were living with the consequences. If we had just had more confidence in our idea from the beginning. If we had just opened a store in King of Prussia at the outset. If, if, if. It didn't do us any good now. All we could do was take it from here. Don't look back.

Nineteen eighty-six was drawing to a close. What a crazy year. It seemed like we were getting back on our feet. At least we had our expenses under control. Somehow we eked out a profit that year. I was losing that sense of panic that had followed me around day and night. We were stable. Waiting for the next opportunity. We knew where we wanted to go. That's always the first step in getting there. The only question now was which road to take. The answer came sooner than we expected.

How to Handle Disasters and Other Unforeseeable Crises—Count on Them!

▼ ▼ ▼

It's not a matter of *if* a disaster occurs. It's a matter of when. Every business will be put to the test at some time or another. By the same token, opportunities will present themselves that you could never have foreseen. And sometimes disasters and opportunities are one and the same. It all depends on how you look at the situation. You can protect yourself from some disasters by planning ahead, buying insurance, and employing redundant systems and backup strategies. Other times you may find yourself dealing with "acts of God, unforeseen conditions, and acts of war," as the fine print says, which are totally unpredictable and impossible to foresee. I'm sorry to say, I have dealt with a myriad of disasters. The most important weapon in dealing with all disasters is maintaining a good mental outlook on life. When you give up, that's when you fail.

Most disasters have a financial impact. That's why it's so important in business to have a cash cushion somewhere. I always had a hard time with this because any cash lying around was always swept into a new initiative, like a new store or more inventory. But as a larger company, we have established the discipline to live within our means, and then some. It is imperative to have either cash or credit available for the unforeseen.

When disaster strikes, you may be devastated, but now more than ever you have to pull yourself together and be a leader for your employees. Remember, they are living with this disaster too. And they have even less control in dealing with it than you do. It is important to communicate to your team the nature of what happened and exactly what you are planning to do about it. Then keep them informed of your progress, good or bad. The worst thing in a disaster is the unknown. Imagination run amok will always be worse than reality.

You may not be able to insure against every eventuality, but there is a minimum level of insurance that is definitely worth your while to invest in. Spend the time with your insurance agent to determine the right policies for your business, using your own good judgment to sort out the worthwhile from the frivolous. For example, fire insurance is obvious. Earthquake insurance? Maybe in San Francisco. Product liability is a judgment call. I never thought I needed it, selling clothes. But a situation arose where I did (see below). And obviously some businesses, such as toy companies and pharmaceutical companies, must have product liability insurance.

There is no way I could cover all the bad things that could

happen to good companies, but I want to make a few comments on my favorite types of disaster.

Fire and Other Natural Disasters

My company has been the victim of fire on three occasions. In addition, we had a store in Los Angeles that was badly damaged by an earthquake, and another one in Miami that was ravaged by a hurricane. In every case we were covered by insurance, and recovered the cost of the physical damage, but the downtime and related disruption to our business was enormous. Physical property must be covered by insurance. The last thing you want to face when dealing with a natural disaster is being underinsured. If you have lenders or investors, they will insist on this to protect their asset. And you should adopt the same attitude. You need to be spending your emotional energy on rebuilding and getting back to normal, not on financial loss. If your claim is substantial, I highly recommend the use of an insurance adjuster. (Just check the yellow pages.) They know the ins and outs of most policies, and they will get you all that you are entitled to. I wouldn't want to go up against an insurance company without one of these guys on my side.

Product Liability

Even the best product can go wrong. In ways you never thought possible. I was caught in a very sad lawsuit many years ago when a manager in one of my stores, unbeknownst to me, was running a side business selling baby sleeping baskets to the maternity customers. A baby died of SIDs while sleeping in one of those baskets, and even though I had never even seen this product before, Mothers Work became involved in the lawsuit because the basket had been sold to this customer while she was in our store. Under the "deep pocket" principle, she included my company in the lawsuit because we were a larger entity than the store manager. Luckily the manager had product liability insurance for her baby basket business, and her insurance company managed the lawsuit. After several years, the lawsuit was settled for a modest amount of money. But this very unfortunate case illustrates just how unpredictable liability can be. If you're in business, you have liability.

Public Relations

The media can blow a situation totally out of control. And you may have very little control over the situation. In the SIDs case, my unfortunate store manager found her house surrounded by TV crews and newspaper reporters one morning as she was leaving for work. She was being portrayed as an unfeeling person, responsible for a tragedy. Luckily she kept her head about her and was able to calmly respond to the media questions. I usually recommend speaking to the media in a crisis. They may have already written their story before they call you, but at least you will have the opportunity to tell your own version. And just being willing to show your face and answer questions honestly and sympathetically is better than a terse "no comment." Sometimes you may even be able to change a reporter's opinion when he or she hears your side. If your company has made a mistake or done something wrong, there is nothing like a good old-fashioned apology. I know that larger companies try to insulate themselves from the media by hiring a PR firm, and if you are so uneasy with the media that you think you'll come off in a negative light, then you should consider it. But the expense for a small company may not be worth it. The best strategy is to communicate honestly and make yourself available to the press.

Computer Crash

Almost everyone is dependent on computers. I know we certainly are. If our computers go down, we are out of business. We have elevated computer redundancy into an art form to protect ourselves. We actually have two mainframe computers either one of which could run the entire company temporarily if the other one went down. We have one on the southeast corner of the building, with telephone lines and power lines from one substation, while the other is on the opposite corner of the building with a different substation's power and a different telephone exchange. If an airplane crashed into our building and took one computer down, the other would survive. We also have all the daily and weekly backup activities you would expect, including off-site data storage. When we first started, Dan and I would personally take a backup tape home every day. We have actually never had a computer crash, and I hope we never do. But if it happens, we'll be ready.

Production Disasters

Recently someone sent me an unsolicited résumé for a job in the garment sourcing and production area. Her résumé said she had turned a production error of a huge quantity of knit shirts, which had been manufactured at a substandard weight, into a business opportunity by negotiating a new cost and selling them through a different distribution channel. In the process she developed a successful ongoing program for her new product. I was so impressed I immediately called her up for an interview. Not only had she acknowledged her mistake, she had turned it to her advantage. That's what you need to do in the face of production problems. They can never be swept under the rug. Worst case, you need to scrap your product and start over. But *never* ship substandard product to your customers. That's the only response that can really kill you.

You will undoubtedly come up with your own disasters. It may be cold comfort to know that everyone else is fighting surprise and random attacks from forces outside of their control. But you will get through it if you are determined and you persevere. And you'll be stronger for it.

Chapter Eight Checklist

▾ Disaster will occur, so it's important to have a cash cushion somewhere.

▾ Insuring your business is a must, if you want to sleep soundly at night.

▾ Product liability insurance is even more of a must.

▾ If your company is caught up in a lawsuit, public relations—having an opportunity to communicate your version of events—is important.

▾ You must have a backup to your computer system, for some day your system might crash.

▾ In the face of production problems, never duck a defect by shipping substandard product to your customers.

chapter nine

Getting to Yes

By the time 1987 rolled around, I was taking my salary again. Dan and I actually took a vacation that year. We went to Club Med in Guadeloupe, and Isaac and Josh stayed with my parents. I remember we bought one of those package deals. Saturday to Saturday. Fixed price, cheap airfare. The first day was fabulous. No kids. No business. On Monday we called the office and talked to Gerta, who had some questions about fabric orders, and got the daily sales flash. Our controller wanted to ask us about some checks and whether he should release them. Our talk on the beach turned to maternity clothes. By the time Wednesday came, our stay on the beach was starting to seem like a jail sentence. *What were we doing here anyway?* Dan had always hated the beach and the sand. We both wanted to get back to work. I called around to the airlines to see when we could get a flight back. Thursday morning we flew home, paying an extra $500 to do so because we had nonrefundable, nonchangeable tickets. I guess you could say we're workaholics, but when you work for yourself, there's no separation between church and state.

It was a relief to get back to work. Back to figuring out how to expand without any available territory. Then came that call from the San Francisco franchisee that moved us off the dime. Did we want to buy the franchise back? I tried to keep the enthusiasm out of my voice.

"Well, I don't know, Kate, what did you have in mind?"

"It's not that we don't love running the store. You know we're making a *lot* of money here. It's just that Virginia and Ted are getting divorced and Virginia needs to liquidate her share. And I've been thinking about going back to work in investment banking because you know I made a *lot* of money in that business. So we're just exploring our options here. And we know that you and Dan want to open more stores."

I told Kate to send me some numbers. I wanted to see the last year or so of her income statement, plus a balance sheet, and decide what I thought it was worth. I hung up the phone and smiled. I had no idea how we were going to pay for it, but I knew I would figure it out.

As soon as I got Kate's information I got to work studying the numbers. I called our bank and asked them if they would help me finance it. They seemed open to the idea, so I got my Lotus 1–2–3 spreadsheet going and made up an analysis that showed how I could buy the store for three times the cash flow being generated by the franchisees and still make enough to pay back the bank if they would lend me the money for the deal. I figured I would pay in cold hard cash, since that would be what I would want if I were Kate. No schedule of payments over time, or shares of Mothers Work stock, or anything else. Just cash. One of the tricks that made the deal work was the fact that I could make more money than Kate because my cost of merchandise was lower. Kate had to buy the product from me, which included a markup for my profit. Whereas, if I sold those same clothes directly through my own store, the cost of the merchandise was much lower. So the additional profit could go toward paying the bank back. And the store would still make a profit even after servicing the debt.

I called my investor to let him know what we wanted to do. Now that we had investors, of course they had to be on board with a major acquisition like this. I figured he'd just say, "Fine, go ahead, great idea." He didn't.

"I think we should take a look at this at the next board meeting," he said. "After all, you've made a great deal of money as a franchiser. Retailing is a different business. Before we buy back a franchise, we need to understand what that means to the future of the business."

I couldn't believe it. I didn't want to wait until the next board meeting. I wanted to do this thing now, before Kate changed her mind. I called my other investor. He liked the idea, but he also wanted to see the numbers. Have a board meeting.

"Well, can we at least have a special board meeting so I don't have to wait? How about tomorrow?" I said. We used to be able to get an idea and go do it. Now I had to sell my partners on it before I could sell the bank on it, and then I had to sell Kate on the deal too. Life was definitely getting complicated.

Eventually we had our special board meeting and showed our investors our idea. They told us to go ahead with the deal. Okay. One hurdle passed. Next I scheduled a meeting with the bank. They liked the idea. Two down. Then I called Kate back and gave her my proposal. Her store had an annual sales volume of $450,000 and a pretax profit of $85,500, excluding depreciation. They had no bank debt. I told her I'd pay three times her EBITDA (earnings before interest, taxes, depreciation, and amortization)—her cash flow. That was a purchase price of $256,500.

The deal looked like this:

Pro Forma Income Statement

	Operated by Franchise	*Operated by Company*
Revenue	$450,000	$450,000
Cost of merchandise	(55%) 247,500	(35%) 157,500
GROSS MARGIN	$202,500	$292,500
Credit card fee	(3%) 13,500	(3%) 13,500
Royalty	(3%) 13,500	
Rent and expenses (including payroll, local ads, etc.)	90,000	100,000
PRETAX INCOME	$85,500	$179,000

PURCHASE PRICE

Three times cash flow generated by franchise:

3 × $85,500 = $256,500

FUNDED BY	
Bank Loan	$200,000
Cash	56,500
TOTAL	$256,500

AVAILABLE FUNDS TO SERVICE BANK DEBT		
Pretax Income as operated by company	$179,000	
First year interest 8%	14,320	
Principal payment	66,667	(paid over three years equal payments)
Remaining cash flow per year after paying bank:	$98,013	

Kate waffled.

"I don't know," she said. "I would never be selling right now if it weren't for Virginia getting divorced. After all the work we put into it, I hate to just walk away from it. And I know you're going to go public down the road. You'll make a killing, and I won't get anything."

I couldn't believe it. After I finally got all my ducks in a row, she was changing her mind. I couldn't pay her more money just because she *wanted* it. I could only pay her what her store was worth. I mean, I had to convince the bank to finance it and I had to get my investors to back it. They were never going to go for it if I went back to them now to increase the purchase price. And even if I got another $50,000 or $100,000 for her, that wasn't what she was really angling for. She wanted a piece of the pie. Even though she was cashing out now, she still wanted to hold on to a piece of the future growth of Mothers Work. After all, she was in the investment banking business. She had seen people make tons of money from growing companies and taking them public.

"Kate, I'll tell you what," I said. "My investors just paid $10 per share to buy into Mothers Work. They expect to sell out one way or another for five or ten times what they paid for it within the next five years." I could hear her salivating. I was getting to her. "I'll give you options to purchase five thousand shares for $10 per share anytime in the next five years. It won't cost you a thing now. But if the shares are worth $100 each when we go public in three years, you can participate. You'd make almost half a million dollars."

She pretended to think about it, but I knew I had her. She accepted almost immediately. I was learning an important lesson about negotiating: figure out what the other side wants. I was giving up very little, but it meant a great deal to Kate. And it was infinitely more persuasive than throwing more money into the pot, which would have been much harder for me to come up with anyway.

When we bought the San Francisco franchise, we bought much more than the downtown store that did $450,000 in sales. We bought a territory with a population of more than 5 million. And we bought access to one of the highest-volume triple-A malls in America, in Palo Alto, just outside of San Francisco.

We needed more money to open more stores. What good was all of this territory and all of these malls if we couldn't take advantage of it and expand?

My next round of investment came from venture capital funds, companies with $10 million or $20 million raised and put into a fund for the purpose of investing in relatively high risk, high-growth companies. Although we already had two private investors, their investments were slightly different because they were investing their own money, along with money from some of their friends and business acquaintances. They were somehow a little less formal. A little more patient. The venture capital funds were more intense and more serious about going public in a clear five-year time horizon. If you couldn't go public, they would want you to be acquired so they could sell out and make big bucks. They euphemistically called it their exit strategy. But you always knew what they really meant. Get big or get sold.

We ended up with two venture capital funds investing a total of about $700,000. One of them was run by a woman who had worn Mothers Work suits while she was pregnant. The Old Girls Network strikes again. Now we had monthly board meetings. Forecasts. Financial reporting. We were under a lot of pressure to grow and make a profit. Of course that's what we wanted too.

We moved our warehouse one more time. We were always running out of space, and we needed a loading dock with a freight elevator. This time we finally decided to consolidate our home second-floor office with the warehouse. Up until then I had kept the order entry and accounting people in our house so I could be closer to Isaac and Josh. Now I would no longer be working at home. Of course I had spent almost every day running over to the warehouse anyway, but now I really had to admit that I didn't work at home. Maybe that's when I got the idea to have another baby. Just to show that I could still be a good mom. Or maybe it was because I was about to turn thirty-five, and I wasn't quite ready to be that old. Or maybe we just *wanted* another baby. Anyway, that's what happened. I got pregnant. Dan would have been happy to have four or five or six kids. My mother was thrilled. And my father—well, he already had shown his proclivities: my parents had six kids themselves.

The only parties who were a little unhappy about my condition were my investors. After all, they had just put more than a combined $1 million into my company. And they didn't want me taking time off having babies. They really didn't have to worry about it. First of all, being pregnant gave me a renewed firsthand customer experience. And second of all, I don't think I actually took more than a morning off. Christina was born on a Friday afternoon. I came home from the hospital on Sunday. And sometime on Monday around two o'clock Dan called and asked if I felt well enough to come over and look at a few design boards. My mother drove me over. Like most moms with kids to be cared for, there's no such thing as downtime.

Plus, I was teaching my investors something. Namely, that babies and motherhood are not necessarily bad for business. Being a mother had trained me in ways that I had never anticipated. Not only could I prioritize and organize better, but I actually believe that my negotiating and managing skills were first learned by running a family and training new human beings. I recently read a quote concerning the skills of mothers who work, from Patricia Fili-Krushel, an executive mom who is the president of the ABC Television Network, and the mother of a six-year-old and an eight-year-old. In response to the question "Does being a mom make me a better manager?" she replied, "Oh yes. It's perfected my negotiating skills." Today she is responsible for all programming, affiliate relations, marketing, and broadcast operations for ABC. Obviously, being the mother of two small children has not slowed her down. Being responsible for another person's life makes a parent mature in fundamental ways. And working parents bring a tremendous set of management skills to the workplace.

I set up a new routine with Christina. Since I was nursing her, she stayed with me all day. We'd bundle her up in the morning and the three of us would drive to our new office. I had a little foam rubber couch in the office that opened up to a bed. I would open it up halfway so it made a four-sided foam rubber nest for her. She was such a happy little baby. I would have meetings and work right around her, and she hardly ever got in the way. I'd haul her all around the office and the warehouse too, nursing right on the spot when I needed to. Even though I was busier than ever with my company, buying franchises and opening stores, Christina seemed to fit into all of our lives without effort. This time around I knew what I was getting into. And I was ready. I knew how to organize my time and fit in my parenting role as well as my business role. And I had worked through my emotional issues, so that I could enjoy my time with my baby and not let guilt overtake me when I wasn't with her. I know that my calmer demeanor made all of our lives easier, including Christina's. Recently in a quiet moment, she turned to me and said, "I want to be just like you when I grow up." I gave her a little hug and tried to contain my exhilaration. I couldn't have asked for more.

After we bought the San Francisco franchise, other opportunities presented themselves. Of course with our new investment we were able to open more stores in our existing territories. For example, we opened in the Palo Alto mall, and that store was an amazing success, just as we thought it would be. We opened in Miami. Then Detroit. And very soon the other franchisees started to make little exploratory calls about selling their businesses back to us. They all saw that Kate and her partners made money and they wanted to get some too. I worked with each franchise to structure a deal that satisfied them. Every one had to be creatively financed. I would make up a financial model and see how much the bank would finance. Then I would close the gap in various ways. Sometimes I would get the franchise to take a note, subordinated to the bank and payable over time. "Subordinated to the bank" simply meant that in case Mothers Work went bankrupt, the liquidation of the company's assets would go to pay back the bank first before any money went to pay back the franchisee note. But as long as we stayed in business, the franchisee would get paid back on schedule.

For several of the purchases we found investors who would put in subordinated debt with stock options or warrants. Because the franchises were all profitable, every time we bought one back we increased our cash flow, so we could afford to take on more debt. The one thing we resisted was giving out more equity. We didn't want to sell more shares, because we all thought that a year or two years later the company would be worth much, much more and we didn't want to dilute our percentage of the total company. So we kept piling on more and more debt—to the bank, to the franchisees, and to various new investors that we brought in. But financing wasn't our only challenge.

In the late eighties fashion started to change for working women. More to the point, fashion came back. The navy-blue-suit look started to take a backseat to fashion, and "soft dressing" became the new look. We had to change our designs to keep up with the style changes, and even our name, Mothers Work, became a liability because it sounded so corporate and limited to suits and work clothes. The Page Boy merchandise was starting to look better and better, and the venture-capital-backed A Pea in the Pod was expanding like crazy. We heard rumors that they were doing more than a million dollars of annual sales in some of their stores. Somehow we had to break into the fashion maternity business.

The ultimate transaction came out of the blue one day and became the maternity fashion entry point that we had been looking for. Like so many opportunities, it was really the culmination of a million events leading up to being in the right place at the right time. And it came in the form of a phone call. The president of Shirley K Maternity called to see if we were interested in acquiring eight Shirley K stores. Shirley K was a Canadian company that had sixty or so maternity stores in Canada as well as eighty or ninety stores for plus-size women. They were a huge public company and dominated the maternity business in Canada. In an effort to keep growing, they had decided to expand into the United States market about three years prior. We watched as they opened eight beautiful stores in big malls in the best markets. Chicago, New York, Boston, and Washington, D.C. My franchisees were getting really nervous about the competition because they came out of nowhere and built these beautiful stores in the best malls. It seemed like money was no object. Well, wasn't it interesting to learn from the president that they never actually made any money in them? They discovered that the U.S. market was different. The clothes that sold in Canada didn't do so well in the United States. And the cost of running eight stores in a foreign country was not being covered by the operations. So as quickly as they had opened them, they were now ready to dump them. What an unbelievable opportunity this was for us. Of course all it required was money.

I knew we had to find a way to acquire Shirley K, USA. Not only would it boost our revenue, it was just the chance we had been searching for to get into the fashion maternity business. We decided that eight stores was the right size to launch a new concept of maternity with a fashion focus. Higher-priced than Mothers Work, and unencumbered with the Mothers Work reputation for career clothes, this would be our competitive answer to Page Boy and A Pea in the Pod. We would carry a whole new line of maternity clothes with a fashion edge, and we decided to change the stores' name from Shirley K to Mimi Maternity, after my sister. Besides, Mimi had a French sound to it, which was the image we wanted to project. The eight Shirley K stores had combined annual sales of over $3.5 million, which would really kick up our size. And, as in the franchise acquisitions, I was able to finance it with mostly debt plus a layer of subordinated debt with warrants. Our total company revenue went from about $7 million to over $11 million instantly on the day we settled the transaction.

The key to negotiating the Shirley K deal was in understanding the other side's need for a quick transaction that allowed them to gracefully exit the United States. They wanted to sell to someone who would take all eight of the stores and continue to operate them, preferably under a new name. That way they could save face with their own shareholders. Selling a going concern looks much better than closing down or selling off the parts to different people. They didn't necessarily have to make a lot of money from the transaction either. It just needed to be clean and quick. We closed the deal less than six weeks after that first phone call. I made sure the documents were drawn up right away. And we were able to do an "asset purchase" rather than a purchase of the corporation. That meant that we just bought inventory, leases, and leasehold improvements. If we found out after the settlement that there was an unpaid bill, or a lawsuit against the company, then that would go back to Shirley K, not us. We didn't accept any liabilities.

The last major franchise that we bought back was Meryl's New York territory. Right to the end, Meryl was my sentimental favorite, and I felt like an era was ending when we went to that settlement. It was eight years since we had negotiated our franchise contract with Mike and Meryl in my mother's greenhouse, four years since that call from the San Francisco franchise offering to sell their business. In that four years we had unwound what had taken us just as long to build. We were a different company now. We were retailers. Vertically integrated retailers.

Mothers Work was ten years old. We had revenues of $19 million in 1992. We were in shooting range of a public offering. Investment bankers were starting to call us out of the blue to see if they could come and present options to us even though the market for initial public offerings (IPOs) was not good in 1992. The market was still nervous, coming out of a recession sparked by the Gulf War. But the bankers knew that it was just a matter of time before things would change. They wanted to be positioned with all the upcoming young companies, ready to pounce when the window for new issues opened up. You never knew when it would open, and you never knew when it would slam shut. So the bankers hovered overhead, waiting. We were now one of those IPO prospects. It was only a matter of time.

The Art of Negotiating

▼ ▼ ▼

I don't want to overemphasize the role that negotiating plays in striking a deal. I truly believe that market forces are much more important, and they usually prevail over any fancy negotiating strategies. By that I mean the overriding influence on any deal is that it must be good for both the buyer and the seller and that the price must be within the range of other, similar deals. When all those things come together, the deal will too. The power of negotiation is in extracting the last 10 percent in your favor. And sometimes good negotiating means finding the right set of conditions that allows the deal to happen at all. Negotiating is an art, not a science. There is no one way or formula that comes out successfully every time. And since negotiating involves people, the best negotiators are the ones who understand the psychology of the deal, and the human factors involved. Here are a few ideas to think about when you are negotiating your next deal.

Be a good listener. The most fundamental skill in negotiating a deal is to understand the other side's motivations. People don't always say what they really mean, so in order to understand, you must not only listen but also interpret what has been said. When I was negotiating to buy the San Francisco franchise, Kate said the price was too low. What she really meant was that she didn't want to give up the chance for stock appreciation down the road if we took the company public. She was looking for future rewards. At first I thought she meant that she wanted more money now. So I wasn't responding to her needs by increasing her current return with a higher purchase price. Once I really *listened,* I understood her true motivation, and then I was able to satisfy it with stock options. Sometimes ego is the driving motivation. The appearance of a good deal may mean more than the actual amount of cash changing hands. For example, if someone selling you her business wanted to believe it was worth more than it really was, you might be able to bridge the gap by offering a percentage of future profits. That way, if things really do work out well, you would both reap the rewards. But if profits never were to materialize, your purchase price would not be too large.

Don't squeeze. Get a good deal, but don't squeeze so hard that you get no deal. Don't overnegotiate. I've seen people talk and talk about making an acquisition, without ever being able to pull it off, because every deal breaks down when they squeeze too hard. The fear of being taken advantage of or the fear of overpaying prevents them from ever closing a deal. Sure, there are times when the deal is too expensive, and the best thing to do is walk away. But if this happens over and over, you may be squeezing too hard.

Never make the first offer. Whether you're buying or selling, try to get the other side to make the first offer. You learn a lot about the other side's state of mind by that first offer. And if you make it yourself, you could easily be way too high or way too low. And once you've stated your offer, it is very hard to back down. When someone says, "What do you want for it?," whether "it" is a house, your business, or an antique vase, the proper response is "Make me an offer."

Set your limit beforehand and don't go over it. In the heat of the moment it is very easy to get carried away and pay too much. There is a maximum price that you can afford and that reflects the value of the deal to you. Figure out what that price is and then don't go over it. You don't want to wake up the next morning with a deal that you can't finance, or one that will never make money for you. If you *have* to have something at any price, whether it's a business or a new house, and you'll do anything to get it, I can almost guarantee you'll pay more than necessary. The other side will know and take advantage of it. Believe me. You can smell it when someone is desperate to make a deal. You simply must be willing to walk away when the deal exceeds the limit you have set for yourself. And if it is a reasonable limit, then ten to one the other side will come back to you. Why would they get more from someone else? Remember, there is a market value, and unless you get emotionally attached to something, and refuse to walk away from a deal that has become overpriced, the market value will usually prevail. So set your limit and stick to it.

Don't bluff. There are only a few people I have ever met who can bluff effectively. They're usually wild and crazy types who are capable of doing anything and can make you believe they *will* do anything, like kill a deal unless you give in to whatever small deal point you happen to be negotiating. For the rest of us, bluffing works only once. Then if your bluff is called, your credibility is totally destroyed.

Let's say you are buying a business and you have agreed to the major terms, like price and form of payment. And maybe you have agreed to pay half in cash and half in the form of a note that you will pay over three years, with 8 percent interest. Now suppose the Federal Reserve lowers interest rates, right in the middle of your deal, and the prime rate goes down by half a percent. You call up the business seller and demand he reduce the interest rate on the three-year note from 8 percent to 7.5 percent. He says no, we already have a deal at 8 percent. You say, things are different now that the prime rate came down half a percent and unless you change your interest rate, the deal's off.

You're bluffing. There's no way you will kill this deal over a half percent interest on half of the purchase price. After all, the difference in what you will pay over the three years is peanuts, but you feel morally correct. The seller feels morally correct too because you already agreed to 8 percent and now you're welching on the deal. But let's say you need the deal more than he does. Maybe he was ambivalent about selling in the first place. He sticks to his guns, and finally you give in. Guess what? The seller now has the advantage on every other little sticking point that comes up. Because now he knows that you will back down. He knows you want this deal more than he does.

It would have been infinitely better if you had accepted his 8 percent but traded for some other small point that you wanted. Maybe you could suggest a three-month moratorium on principal and interest payments—in other words, wait three months after settlement before you start making the payments—to give you time to save up some cash. Or maybe there is another small point you could try to resolve in your favor. Just remember, bluffing can backfire. And it usually does.

Patience pays. A sense of urgency in business is essential. The successful entrepreneur knows that tomorrow is too late for whatever can be done today. However, there are times in negotiating a deal when patience is more than a virtue; it is a necessity. Sometimes I think that venture capitalists are taught in business school to drag their feet when negotiating every investment. They all seem to do it. And if you're running out of money and dying for that investment, time is on the side of the investor. With every passing day, you become more desperate to get the deal done, and you are more willing to give in on every point just to get your hands on some money. Now, obviously every company is not running out of money during every venture capital negotiation, but the principle remains. Patience in a deal shows strength. It's important to expedite a deal, but if the other side seems to be foot-dragging on purpose, then just be ready to slow down and not show your anxiousness, or you might be showing your need to do the deal, which would exhibit weakness.

Never be emotional even if the other side is. Screamers rarely win in the end. Never be intimidated by this silly tactic. I have seen people get up and leave the room when the other side engaged in an emotional screaming fit. Leaving the room was a very effective move, and the screamer was left looking juvenile and had to apologize later.

Always have a key decision maker behind the scenes. There is a very funny part in an Italian godfather type of a movie where the head gangster breaks off a negotiation to consult with his father, the head of the family, before he can render his final decision. The black limo takes him to a guarded estate where he goes to the garden to speak to his father. After a minute of listening to the gangster making his case, we see that the father is in a wheelchair, totally incapacitated, mentally as well as physically. And that the gangster is actually talking to himself. Why does he need this ruse? Because keeping the decision maker behind the scenes gives him the power to delay decisions, think them over, or even change his mind. All with the pretext of needing to check with the "real" boss. You need a real boss behind the scenes too. I used to use my board of directors all the time. Or Dan, or even my financier, the bank, whatever. Then the board of directors or the bank can turn things down if you don't want to give in to a certain point. Never put yourself forward as the ultimate decision maker. Just the main one.

Once you practice negotiating, you will develop your own style. These rules, and others, will become second nature. The final thing I want to say on this subject concerns integrity in negotiating a deal. A negotiation is a series of back-and-forth discussions, where you work issues through one at a time. Often, there will be a give and then a take, almost requiring a scorecard. It is imperative that both sides be able to trust each other to keep their word on each point that is won or lost, so that when you reach the end, and it's up to the lawyers to document the deal you struck, neither side tries to go back and change one or two points, or forget that one side agreed to back down from one deal point in order to get another. The whole deal could start to unravel if this happens. If you don't have a great memory for small details, take notes of your conversations as they happen, highlighting the key points of the negotiation. You must be true to your word to be a good negotiator.

Chapter Nine Checklist

- To negotiate a deal successfully, be a good listener. Try to understand what motivates the other person.
- Don't squeeze so hard that you lose the deal.
- Never make the first offer.

- ▾ Figure out what your price limit is in advance—and then don't go over it.
- ▾ Attempts to bluff will usually backfire.
- ▾ Patience is not only a virtue—in negotiating, it can be a necessity.
- ▾ Keep a key decision maker behind the scenes.
- ▾ Integrity—and trust—are essential in bringing a deal to completion.

chapter ten

Going Public

The summer of 1992 was one of the worst environments for new issues, meaning initial public offerings (IPOs). The country was coming out of a recession, and the risk of investing in new public companies was one that investors were not willing to take. Despite the recession, our sales and profits were strong that year. Looking back, I can now see why. During 1992 our country had an unusually high number of births. In fact, 1992 was one of the handful of years in the history of the country that saw more than 4 million births. We tried to take advantage of our strong numbers, which exceeded most retailers' results at the time, by speculating that since unemployment was up, unemployed women were taking the opportunity to start a family, being in between jobs. After all, what better time was there for a professional woman to have a baby than when she was out of work? Of course investors and other Wall Street types *loved* that explanation, because everyone is always looking for the perfect "recession-proof" company to invest in. And since, at the time, we couldn't really *know* why our sales were up, this was a plausible explanation, and we believed it.

In retrospect, it became evident that the summer of '92 was the beginning of the recovery, and since people were starting to feel better about the future, they started having babies again. This theory is borne out by looking at housing starts for 1992. Following more than six years of declining housing starts, that year was the first to see an increase in new construction, a trend that has continued through the present. When you look at the uptick in our revenue along with the uptick in housing starts, you could deduce that revenue trends in our company are a leading indicator of the economy. But whatever the reason, we had a bang-up finish to the year, and it put us in the perfect position to launch an IPO when the market turned around late that year.

One of our board members was an investment banker based in Philadelphia. He called us one day in December and told us that if we wanted to go public, the time was now. The window was open. In the months to come, he became my ally, my friend, and my mentor as the IPO took over my life. Thank God I had someone to turn to at those times when nothing made any sense, and I didn't have a clue what the rules were.

Going public involves compiling a great deal of accounting records, dating back at least three years. Investors want to know all they can about a company when it first goes public. And the Securities and Exchange Commission requires the company to prepare an offering memorandum that discloses not only its accounting records but lots of additional data similar to what you would put into a business plan. When you put together the offering memorandum, the guts of it are the historical financial information and the past and current balance sheets of the company. Investors in public companies want to know dollars and cents. And they aren't about to believe company management. They want to see financial statements audited by a certified public accounting firm. Since we had been a franchiser for almost ten years, we had been required by the Federal Trade Commission to have our financial statements audited for that whole time. This was a big advantage when it came time to go public, because if you don't have them, going back over three years' time and trying to audit financial statements retrospectively can be enormously time-consuming, expensive, and difficult. We called up our accountant and told him we wanted to go public right away. He didn't think twice. "I'm ready," he said.

After years and years of hard work and painstakingly slow progress, things were moving into warp speed. When the window opens, you have to jump. My professional advisers knew this. They had been through it a thousand times before. Some companies wait but are never able to catch the wave—that moment in time when Wall Street is receptive to IPOs and the Dow Jones average is moving up; when your own company is in an up cycle, with good P&L performance; when your particular industry is in favor with investors; and when your revenue is big enough to handle the expense of a public offering. When all the stars align, you have a short period of time to take advantage of it. I have a mental image in my mind of being on the beach and someone yelling "Surf's up!" and all my professionals grabbing their surfboards and running into the water to catch the big one. That's what going public is like.

We knew that the owners of our foremost competition, A Pea in the Pod, were on the same wavelength. After all, they were venture-capital-backed as well. Of course we had no real knowledge of their revenue or profits, since, like us, they were a private company. But the last thing in the world we wanted to happen was to have them go public before we did, because then our future would be controlled by their performance. Wall Street would use them as a comparable company in evaluating us, since there really was no other public maternity company. If they hiccuped, we would be judged. Investors tend to have industry outlooks. "The auto industry is down." Or "The steel industry is being hurt by imports." Or "The maternity industry is experiencing slow growth." Best to just rush out there and *be* the industry. Furthermore, if we were able to get millions of dollars of capital, we'd have armaments in the maternity arms race. We would be able to grab space in the remaining triple-A malls before they could. And sometimes once a mall had one upscale maternity store, a second was superfluous. So getting into the great malls was much easier if you were the first. Between leasehold improvements and inventory, it could require $200,000 or $300,000 to open a new store in a mall. Going public had an urgency for us beyond just cashing out our investors.

We had a board meeting in early January and made the decision to go forward. The next step was interviewing investment bankers, which we started almost the next day. Although our offering wasn't large enough to attract the really big national players, like Merrill Lynch or Smith Barney, we had a surprisingly good reception from the regional investment bankers. My board member, who was also an investment banker, helped us identify about a half dozen firms, and when we contacted them they were all interested in meeting with us. These firms have enough experience to know which companies are ready to go public. They're not about to waste their time flying around talking to companies that don't have the requisite financial track record. Just the fact that so many of them were after our business was an endorsement in itself and gave us the confidence to keep going in the process.

In dealing with investment bankers, it's hard to know who is interviewing whom. On the one hand, the bankers will make a lot of money from the transaction, so they should be trying to impress you with their expertise and IPO track record. But on the other hand, the bigger and more prestigious the firm, the choosier they are. They have a reputation to maintain with the institutions that do the stock buying in an IPO, and they are putting their stamp of approval on your company if they take it public. A little mating dance ensues where each one attempts to gain the upper hand. You ask: "Tell me what companies you have taken public recently. Did they have successful offerings? Did their stock sell at a high price? And do you have relationships with lots of institutional buyers who will want to buy my stock?" (Institutional buyers are the key to a successful stock offering. They are the big money market funds, the insurance companies, and the pension funds that have billions of dollars to invest and that participate in almost all of the IPOs. Every investment banking firm tries to cultivate their business.) Their response usually goes something like this: "How can we know that you will make your profit forecasts next year after we take you public?"

In other words, they don't want to be embarrassed when your stock drops, after selling it to lots of institutional buyers, because of your bad performance.

Our first interview didn't go so well. My board member had set it up. Harry, a well-dressed man in a pinstriped suit and manicured fingernails from a well-known firm which shall remain nameless, showed up at our office with his team one Monday morning. His team consisted of three Harry wannabes: a retail industry specialist, an account executive who would be assigned to our offering, and an assistant. They were all equally well groomed. Harry exuded confidence and had the kind of personality that demanded your attention. Dan and I were waiting in our conference room when Harry burst onto the scene. I held out my hand, but he walked right by me toward Dan and grabbed his hand and shook it.

"Glad to be here," he said. He looked around and saw me, and gave me a smile. "Could I get some coffee?" he asked.

Dan suppressed a smile. He knew this guy was getting to me before we had even sat down. "This is Rebecca," Dan said. "She's the president of our company."

Harry whirled around and looked at me, obviously taken aback. But being the pro that he was, he rebounded immediately. "Glad to meet you!" he boomed.

"The pleasure's mine. What would you like in your coffee?" I was trying to stay above it all, ignoring his obvious tendencies toward what we used to call "male chauvinist pig." But I couldn't believe that he would fly all the way out to see us and not know who the president of the company was. His lack of preparation got on my nerves even more than his sexism.

We all sat down at the conference table. First Harry and his team gave a sales pitch for their company, listing off all the recent IPOs they had managed and talking about their exhaustive knowledge of the retailing industry and why they were the obvious and best choice to be the underwriters of our offering. Then Dan and I talked about Mothers Work, how I had started the company after experiencing a market void for career maternity clothes, what our recent revenue growth had been, and so forth. When we had finished exchanging information, Harry cleared his throat and puffed himself up, getting ready to make a little speech.

"Dan," he began, looking right at Dan, "Rebecca," he continued, making eye contact with me, "I've been in the investment banking business a long time. And I can tell you that the market for IPOs is heating up. You have a great company here, and I think I can help you. But the key to a successful IPO is *perception.*" He jabbed his finger at us to make his point. "You could have the greatest company in the world, but if it isn't *perceived* that way, then it doesn't matter."

I had no idea what he was talking about, but I waited for him to finish.

"You *do* want to get the best offering price you can, right?"

We nodded.

"Well, the way to accomplish that is to enhance your *perceived* value. Investors are looking to the president to lead the company into the future and increase the price per share. And so the *perception* of the president is utmost in people's minds. Now, what I suggest is that Rebecca step down as president and Dan be the president so that you'll have a better road show. After all, most of the investors are men. They will relate better to a man as president."

We stared at him.

"Hell, for all I care you can switch your titles back after the road show."

Was this man serious? Was he right? Would we really get a better price per share if Dan were the president? I was stunned that he would suggest such a ridiculous move, but on the other hand, he did have a lot of experience taking companies public. I didn't want to jeopardize our offering just because of my ego, if he really knew something I didn't. I wasn't sure what to say. Coming out of my ruminations, I realized that Dan was speaking.

". . . and obviously we want to do the right thing. So tell me something. When was the last time that you actually took a company public with a woman president?"

"Well, actually, I, well . . . I, actually I never did."

"Then what makes you think it would be a bad idea?" At least Dan was retaining his sense of logic.

Harry puffed himself up again. "Dan, I know my customers," he said, jabbing his finger again for emphasis. Cornered, with no real facts, evidence, or even credibility, Harry was falling back on intimidation and self-importance. Dan winked at me and began drawing the meeting to a close.

"We'll be contacting you later," he said.

I was doing a slow burn. *Yeah, don't call us, we'll call you.* If this was what going public was going to be like, then maybe it wasn't for us. We wrapped up the meeting and Dan showed Harry and his team to the door. I kicked off my shoes and waited for him to come back to the conference room. He was grinning.

"Beck, don't take that guy so seriously. Not every investment banker is going to be such a jerk."

"I hope so," I said, shaking my head. "I really hope so."

The funny thing is that out of the next five investment bankers we interviewed, not one of them ever mentioned the idea of Dan becoming the president. The subject never came up. No one else thought that a woman president was a liability to the offering. And eventually we had a number of investment bankers who were interested in us, who were well-respected firms and who had superior teams, not lunatics like Harry and his team. We made our choice, with the help of our board members, based not only on the prestige level of the firm but also on the bankers as people and the chemistry between all of us. After all, we would be spending a lot of time together in meetings, and on the road, and the people factor was enormously important. We had to have confidence in their judgment and belief in their abilities. And we had to know that if the offering ran into trouble and was hard to sell, they would redouble their efforts and get it done, instead of dropping us like hot potatoes. We relied on how they conducted themselves in other offerings, and we interviewed a lot of those companies to get confirmation. In hindsight we made a great choice, and we have stayed with the same firm for other banking needs since we have been public.

Then the drafting sessions began. These consisted of all-day meetings with twenty people around a big table. All of the investment bankers would be there with their lawyers, and our accountants were there, and our lawyers, and everybody had assistants. The final product of the drafting sessions was the offering memorandum that was given to investors, describing the company, its history, its financials, the officers and board of directors, and so forth. I can remember one night at 8:30 P.M., when we were all getting really punchy, we got into a big argument about the use of the word "augment." Dan ran out to the bookstore and bought a thesaurus, and then we spent another hour trying to prove who was right.

One day in the middle of a drafting session, our lawyer pulled me and Dan aside and said we were going to have a special meeting. The three of us went into a side room, where the head investment banker and his head lawyer were waiting, looking very serious. We all sat down. The head lawyer cleared his throat. "This is part of the due diligence process," he said. Due diligence means fact-finding. The bankers have an obligation to verify what the company tells them through their own analysis and study so that they aren't knowingly misleading the investors who buy our stock. We waited for him to continue. Finally the head banker looked at us and said, "How's your marriage?"

So that's what this was about. Dan and I relaxed a little and looked at each other. I had to bite my tongue to keep from snickering. After all, this was serious business. They really had a hang-up about this marriage thing. It didn't seem to matter how many successful couples there were in the apparel industry such as Liz Claiborne and her husband, who worked together for years, or Donna Karan, whose husband was the cofounder and vice-chairman of the company. I wanted to tell them to just get over it. But Dan quipped that he had lived with his mother-in-law for six years. "Didn't that pass the test?" he asked. That seemed to satisfy them.

The whole drafting process culminated with the printing of the memorandum, which is an all-night affair, conducted at the office of the financial printer. The lawyers and the investment bankers have to be there for the whole night to check the document as it comes off the press to see that every number is right. There is so much financial liability and money at risk in the IPO process that every word matters. Dan and I finally went home around midnight.

The heart of the IPO is the road show, which starts after the SEC approves the offering memorandum and lasts for about two weeks. The bankers take the company management, usually the president and the CFO, around the country to the major cities, to visit big institutional investors and let them ask questions about the company. As you go from city to city, the salespeople from the investment banking firm take orders for the stock, which will be sold at the end of the road show. Some of the meetings are "one-on-ones," which means you go to a particular investor's office and explain your company to him or her individually. Usually every day there will be a lunch where you make the presentation with a slide show while everyone is eating a rubber chicken special. Most road shows start in California and make their way east, ending up in New York with a large unruly crowd of Wall Streeters, and then Boston, where the big money market funds are based.

When you start the road show, you present a range of possible prices to the investors. In our case the range was $11 to $13 per share. Then after two weeks of making your pitch to the institutions, you get an idea of exactly where the stock should be priced, based on how much interest there is in your company and how much the institutional investors are willing to pay per share. On the last day of the road show, you talk it over with the investment banker and the delegated board members and together make the decision about where to price the offering. If you think there is enough demand for your stock, you can price it near the top of the range. But if you guess wrong, and your price is too high, then the share price usually falls when you actually start trading on the open stock market. That's the last thing the investment bankers want to see, because the institutions that just bought the initial placement, based on the road show, would take an immediate hit. And then the next time the investment banker takes a company on the road, he might lose some credibility.

Ideally the investment bankers want to end the road show with orders for five or six times more stock than they have to sell. They want to go back to each institutional investor and say, "Sorry, you ordered fifty thousand shares, but I can only sell you five thousand because this is such a hot stock." That way, there will be a lot of buy pressure on the stock the minute it hits the public trading floor, and hopefully the price will skyrocket. It's all a crazy process of everyone trying to psych each other out. But underlying it all is a market driven by supply and demand which culminates with that pricing moment, right before the stock is actually sold, and then released to trade in the stock market.

The road-show presentation is a carefully scripted thirty-minute company overview, with another half hour for questions. We rehearsed it a thousand times before we set out, and I had my part practically memorized, including when to be animated and when to be somber. I never strayed from my lines. Dan, on the other hand, used to improvise and experiment with his part. We never knew exactly what he would say. I talked numbers and money, while Dan talked concepts and strategy. Ours was what Wall Street calls a story stock. For the same reason reporters always liked to write about Mothers Work, investors could relate to the story of my company and how it grew from nothing to $19 million in revenue, filling a market void. Many of the investors were women in their thirties who understood the market. And everyone appreciated the concept of a niche market that bigger companies shied away from.

The road show itself was grueling, with sixteen-hour days and sometimes cramming in two and even three cities in one day. We were scheduled to wind up in Boston on a Monday, March 15, with a series of meetings with the big money market funds. These firms are huge players in the IPO market, and no investment banker will price a deal before making the Boston presentations. Dan and I were scheduled to fly up to Boston Sunday afternoon. We weren't taking any chances on delayed flights or other travel problems. As luck would have it, the coming week was spring break for the kids' school, and we had long ago arranged a family ski trip in the Rockies, with reservations and airfare from Saturday to Saturday. Of course there was no way to get around our being in Boston on Monday, so we asked my mother to fly the kids out and stay with them until we could meet them there Monday night. On Saturday night it started to snow. When we woke up on Sunday, it was looking like a blizzard. We got an early start to the airport, hoping they wouldn't close it before our flight left. We walked in and looked at the arrival/departure board. Every flight read "canceled." This couldn't be happening. It was like they stamped "canceled" right through my IPO. The timing in an offering is critical. If we didn't get to our Boston meetings, it might be impossible to regroup those investors in a meaningful time. And once you launched a road show, if you didn't conclude it within two, *maybe* three weeks, it would spoil like a piece of overripe fruit. The market might change, investors would forget about your stock, and the whole thing would fall apart.

We didn't know it then, but the March 14 blizzard went down in history as one of the biggest on the East Coast ever. It was clear that driving to Boston was out of the question. In good weather, it was an eight-hour trip. I wasn't even sure we would be able to drive home from the airport at this point. The only other possibility was the train. We ran to the airport train station. Then we waited. And waited. Finally, amazingly, a train limped up to the platform. Now we were getting somewhere. It was a slow, agonizing train ride to 30th Street Station in Philadelphia, and it was snowing so hard you couldn't see more than ten inches in any direction. The minute we set foot in the train station I could tell that it was a hopeless cause. It was packed with travelers, loaded down with big bags. They were going nowhere. And we were too. We turned around and went back to the airport. Out of options, we called our investment banker at home and told him there was no way we could get to Boston. He said he would send the company plane to get us there the next morning as soon as the runways were cleared. We stayed in the airport hotel that night.

It seemed ridiculous. To come so far and then lose it. What if it didn't stop snowing? What if they didn't clear the runway in time? We got up extra early the next morning. Thank God the sun was shining. We needed to get to the private-plane hangar, but there was only one hotel bus in operation and there was a mob of people trying to get on it. Everyone was desperate to get to their flights. One was on a honeymoon. Another was visiting her mother in Iowa. *But we had to go public.* Couldn't they understand that? Somehow we fought our way onto the bus. We drove by mountains of snow and long ugly lines of people trying to check their bags and make their flights.

Even though Boston had been hit by the storm, they were better able to cope with it. Our meetings all went well, and we finished the last one late in the afternoon. We had set up a conference call with our attorney, two of our board members, and the head trader at our investment banker's headquarters to strategize. All through the road-show process the head trader had been keeping track of the orders for our stock, as well as the other investment banks that wanted to be part of the syndicate. (The syndicate is a group of other investment banks that come into the deal to sell shares to their own customers. The bigger your syndicate, the better.) We were told that our offering was being extremely well received and that we had almost eleven times the number of orders as we had shares to sell. Not only that, we had a huge list of investment banks that wanted to be in the syndicate. He started reeling off the list, concluding that we could price the stock at the top of our range. Of course every dollar of price per share represented a huge increase in the amount of money that came into our company. Someone on the call suggested we go above the range. Go to $14, or even $15, per share. Why not? We had a huge demand for our stock. In the end, we decided to stay at $13. We had given the range careful consideration and felt that that was what the stock was worth. If it traded up in the open market, then so be it.

At that moment we pulled up to the front of the airport, at our gate. Dan and I jumped out of the limo and grabbed our bags out of the back. I threw my high heels in the trunk and changed into sneakers. Dan changed into cowboy boots. We put on our down ski jackets and left our overcoats in the trunk. "Send that stuff to my office," I yelled through the car window. We had twenty minutes to make our flight. Off we ran.

As it turned out, we raised $19 million in our offering. About $12 million went to the company, and the other $7 million to our investors who sold some of their shares. Of the $12 million the company received, $5 million went to pay off all the debt we had accumulated in the acquisitions we had made, and the rest went into our company's bank account.

As a public company, Mothers Work went from $19 million in revenue to $300 million in a five-year period of time. I doubt that we would have had the resources to accomplish that as a private company. And as a result, Mothers Work is the largest apparel manufacturer in Philadelphia and the largest maternity retailer in the country. Our company has created employment for over 3,500 people who are directly employed by Mothers Work, and thousands more who do the contract manufacturing in companies all over Pennsylvania and the country. Many of us at Mothers Work are working mothers as well as working fathers. I am not the only one who has found a peaceful coexistence between the two passions of my life: business and family. Despite the challenges of being public, it was the right choice for us, and my greatest hope is that I can inspire others to follow their dreams also.

IPOs, The Street, a Private Jet, and Realizing Your Dream

It's the American dream. It was my dream. Start a company, grow it, and take it public. The character of your company will change once it is publicly traded. Some changes you will like, and others—well, you may want to be careful what you wish for. I will give you the flavor of what it is really like to be a public company and what it takes to get there. Then you can decide if this is *your* dream.

What Does It Mean to Go Public?

First of all, the act of going public will not make you rich. It will only recognize whatever value there already was in your company and give you a way to immediately turn part of it into cash. So the single most important requirement of going public is to build a company that is worth something. What does it mean to "go public"? Let me start with the basic concept of equity. Your company is a separate entity owned by a group of people. If it is a corporation, the owners hold shares of stock, called equity, which entitle them to a piece of the company. If the company is sold outright, the proceeds are used to first pay back debt, then the remaining amount of money is split between the stockholders in proportion to the amount of stock they hold. The total amount of outstanding shares is not important. What is important is the percent of the total number of shares that a single person has. So, for example, if there are 100 shares issued by your company, Acme Tires and Batteries, and you own 20 of them, or 20 percent, that has the same value as if there were 100,000 shares issued and you owned 20,000 of them. In both cases, you own 20 percent of Acme, and if the company were sold for $1 million, you would receive $200,000. In the first case, if there were 100 shares, the price per share would be $1 million divided by 100, or $10,000 per share, and in the second case, if there were 100,000 shares issued, the price per share would be $10.

Now, let's say you take Acme Tires and Batteries public. If you only had 100 shares, the investment bankers would immediately get you to do a 1,000-to-1 stock split, because they like to keep the initial price range between $10 and $15. So your attorney will do a legal filing, and every share splits into 1,000 shares. We can now go to the example of 100,000 shares in the company, worth $10 per share, of which you own 20,000. The process of going public involves registering some of the shares of the company with the Securities and Exchange Commission (SEC). Once those shares are registered, they can be freely traded by the public. Until your stock is registered with the SEC, you can't just go around selling shares.

You have to abide by certain federal laws and rules that protect ordinary people, who are not financially savvy, from being cheated out of their money. Even in a private transaction, such as when you sell your stock to venture capitalists or private investors, you are required to disclose certain financial information about the company. And the investors must represent that they are financially sophisticated, which gets around the need to register the shares with the SEC. One way to prove you are financially sophisticated is by having a high net worth.

But once you have gone through the arduous procedure of registering your shares, which includes writing the offering memorandum, auditing your financials for three years, and so forth, and then having a public offering, those shares can be freely traded on the stock market. Usually in the IPO you will register some of the existing shares already issued to you and your investors, as well as some shares that are newly authorized by the company. The stock offering will be a combination of those shares you and your investors register (and obviously that money goes to the selling shareholders) plus the newly authorized shares that were registered (that money goes to the company). The investment banker makes the final decision about how much stock the selling shareholders can contribute to the offering. He will usually limit that amount so it won't look like all the original owners are dumping their stock and have no future incentive to make the company grow and prosper. After the IPO, you and your investors can sell more of your stock, subject to limits on how much and when. The investment banker will get your agreement on a period of time, say ninety days, when you won't trade any stock, to give adequate time to the market to be unaffected by your selling shares.

Then the SEC will limit your trades in every three-month period to a small percent of the total amount of shares outstanding.

Advantages of Going Public

I think we can all agree that the biggest advantage of going public is that you and your company will get a lot of money. Not only that, you will gain liquidity. You can sell more of your shares in the future, if you need to raise cash, although you are constrained as to how much you can sell in any three-month period. And once you have made an initial offering, if your company requires more capital, it will be much easier to do a follow-on offering, as long as the company is doing well at that time and the price per share is strong. You can use your stock almost like cash when it comes to making acquisitions or doing other deals. And very important, you can give stock and stock options to your key employees or even to all of your employees. There is no better way to have your team all working toward the same goal and focusing on the growth and health of the entire company, instead of their own particular department or area. And since the trading on the stock market is listed every day in the newspaper, the whole team always knows how they are doing. Finally, being public will enhance your company's prestige and visibility. Your suppliers and customers, and even your employees, will see your company as stronger and more important. As head of a consumer company I found this made a real difference. Since investors all over the country knew about Mothers Work, our product was more widely known.

Challenges in Going Public

As a public company the legal, accounting, and investor relations aspects of business become far more expensive and complicated. Given the expense of going public, and then maintaining a public company, a certain revenue volume is necessary. And the time you will have to spend on your new duties can be more onerous than the money required. In our case, as a franchiser who was venture-capital-backed, we had already learned to deal with a complicated legal structure and a strenuous reporting obligation to our investors. We were also used to having investors who had a large stake in the well-being of the company and wanted some say in its operations. If you haven't gone through this process, you will quickly confront the reality of sharing the ownership of the company.

As a public company you will have very real legal and business responsibilities to your shareholders. One of those responsibilities is to constantly keep your shareholders informed of major events. They are entitled to know anything that has an impact on the price per share or the health of the company. And you must inform all the shareholders at the same time, without favoring any, such as your venture capitalists or your friends. No one has special privileges, unless they are on the board of directors, and then they have much more responsibility that goes along with it.

There will be pressure from the investment community to grow the revenue and profit of the company every year. If you don't have a desire to grow your company, it may not be appropriate for you to go public. And finally your company and to some extent your financial information will be available to all. Life in a fishbowl may take some getting used to. Things like your personal salary and ownership percent may be published in the local newspaper. And your competitors will have access to a substantial amount of company information.

Life as a Public Company

In your new life after the IPO, your primary duty remains the same: grow the profitability of your company. It is your job to set the strategy balancing short-term and long-term considerations, as well as the needs of your multiple constituencies, including your shareholders, your employees, and the community. And the fact that you are a public company shouldn't change any of that. What will change is your responsibility to your new shareholders, and the communications to them. Stock analysts from the investment banking firms are one of the means of communicating. The firm that underwrote your public offering has an obligation to the institutional clients who bought the stock to continue providing financial analysis of the company. Your analyst will publish reports updating your condition after major events occur and after earnings releases are made. He or she will want to visit you periodically to stay informed of the company's progress. Over time, other analysts from other firms may want to cover your company as well, as a service to their clients. Analysts usually cover a specific industry, such as retailing or high tech, and as such they are very knowledgeable resources for you as well as a communication pipeline to your shareholders. Your reporting requirements will revolve around your quarterly earnings press releases, and in some industries like retailing, monthly sales releases. Most companies have a quarterly conference call that is made available to all shareholders to discuss the results of the quarter. There are also ongoing quarterly and annual reports made to the SEC, which your accountant and lawyer will help you prepare.

Another thing that takes some getting used to as a public company is the need for confidentiality, and the sensitivity to insider knowledge and how and when to disseminate it to the public. Once upon a time, when you were private, and your friends asked how business was doing, you could respond honestly, describing whatever acquisition you might happen to be working on, or making an accounting of how tough sales might be that month. Now, however, all of that information is insider information and has to be reported to all shareholders and the public at the same time, in the same manner, so that select individuals do not unfairly profit by trading your stock based on such information. A month that has "tough sales" could cause the share price to go down. So if sales are that bad, all of your shareholders need to know. On the other hand, if the month isn't over, sales may turn around by month's end. You can't be making a daily announcement on sales. You need to wait until there is a clear trend and then use judgment as to whether it is material enough to announce. But in the meantime, when your friend asks, "How's business?," maybe you should change the subject.

Chapter Ten Checklist

▾ By going public, you and your company will get a lot of money and gain liquidity.

▼ You can use stock to make acquisitions, and offer options to key employees to keep them from leaving.

▼ As a public company, you have a responsibility to your shareholders, including keeping them informed of major events.

▼ As a public company, financial information about it will be available for all and the financial community will expect to stay informed of your progress.

Epilogue

There had never been another moment in my business life when so much came together at one time than when we took our company public. All of our hard work, mistakes, and good fortune came together in that one moment in time. I thought back to all the early days of tedious, slow progress. The dinners at Friendly's when Dan urged me on. The exploratory trips to New York with Isaac nursing at my breast. The garments that were sewn wrong. The rat-infested warehouse. Then I thought about the small victories. The first order. The first franchise. The revenue milestones. The acquisitions. I had been so busy doing, I never had time to see what I had done. And for the first time, I allowed myself a small self-congratulations.

Of course, going public wasn't an end, but rather the beginning of a whole new chapter in the life of Mothers Work. About six months after we went public, our rival A Pea in the

Pod did the same. And one and a half years after that, in the spring of 1995, we acquired them. We made a few other acquisitions, and somewhere along the way we reorganized into three divisions: A Pea in the Pod (high-priced designer level), Mimi (contemporary), and Motherhood (everyday low price). Every division now carries a full selection of casual and career maternity clothes within its own price/fashion area. We dropped Mothers Work as a store name and changed those stores into one of the three other surviving brands. Now Mothers Work is simply the parent name of the entire corporation.

With over 3,500 employees in more than six hundred stores around the country, I am sad to say that there are many talented and dedicated members of the Mothers Work team that I have never even met. What a change from the early days of me and Lena packing up catalog orders and handing them to the UPS man every night. Needless to say, my management skills required some development along the way. The transition from doing a task to supervising someone else doing that same task is always a hard one for us entrepreneurs. We want to do everything ourselves. But obviously I couldn't be in six hundred stores at once! So delegating, and building a team of other managers who also delegate, were crucial steps in my training. I had to learn to accomplish things through other people so that I could leverage my own efforts. My primary job now is motivating others. Because their success is also my own.

We tried branching out into the fashion business (nonmaternity) with the acquisition of a group of stores called Episode. But after trying to make it profitable for two years, we decided that we were better off focusing our resources and attention in the area that we knew best, maternity. So we closed the Episode stores, and now we are exclusively in the maternity business. But I'll never stop trying, testing, and evolving our business, because when you stand still you become stale and out of date, and some new entrepreneurial company will doubtless run over you.

A few years ago Dan and I finally bought our own house and moved out of my parents' apartment. Now we live next door to them, and they're still a big part in my life and the lives of my children. At least once every few weeks my daughter sleeps over at her grandparents' house, just to keep in touch. And we still have dinner together once a week.

My children are growing up to be independent and confident individuals, and every year I enjoy them more. Although the time requirements of being a mom are easing a little, the emotional and intellectual demands of adolescents and teenagers are enormous. Teaching, coaching, and motivating have supplanted diapers and bake sales. We still have our six o'clock dinner hour religiously, and it is during that time that a lot of problem solving and bonding occurs. Most important, I think that Dan and I have made them know that they are loved and that they can always count on us to help them through life.

As for my own development, I have grown beyond being a quitter. I've learned to trust my own abilities and actually live out the "never give up" rule. Having experienced failure and adversity, I've seen that if you live to fight another day, you can overcome your setbacks and reverse your defeats. I've become stronger because of it. Having Dan as my partner and teacher has bolstered my success beyond measure, but mostly he helped me believe in myself, as surely as your success will come from within you. Every person with entrepreneurial leanings needs people in their life who support their dreams, but ultimately you have to discover your own advantages and then use them. The odds of success are determined by your efforts and refusal to let others discourage your dreams.

Mothers Work is a much more stable company now, and I could probably work less than I do, but the fact of the matter is I don't *want* to. I love what I do. Yet what I love most now is being invited to speak to entrepreneurial groups whose members are just starting their own companies. The energy and creativity that radiate from these gatherings always seems to renew my own drive. A while back, I spoke at a large group of businesswomen at a luncheon. Many had either started their own business or were planning to do so. As I took the podium and looked out at the audience, I remembered the time I had listened to Debbie Fields deliver the keynote speech to a similar group when I was just starting my business. She had been such an inspiration to me then. I wanted to invigorate this group the same way. I wanted them to see their future in Technicolor. I knew that if a single person in the audience were to expand her horizons and believe in her abilities because of what I said, then I would have completed the cycle. As I told my story I emphasized the importance of persevering over a long period of time, and I encouraged them to dream big and believe they could realize their goals.

After my speech a petite woman came up to me and told me that she was thinking about starting her own business as a caterer. She was a new mom and had been saving up to quit her job as a chef, and she had come to hear me speak to reinforce her decision. I wished her luck, and she gave me her card. I had all but forgotten about her until recently when I ran across her business card while flipping through my Rolodex. I immediately recognized her name because she now owns one of the most successful new restaurants in the city. I felt enormously proud of her and happy to know that she had taken steps toward achieving her goal. Every time I drive by her restaurant, I smile to myself.

If you take anything away from this book, I hope it is the inspiration to think big, focus, and never give up. After all, if a maternity power suit was such a good idea, why hadn't someone else thought of it?

MothersWork Business Plan Contest

There are hundreds and even thousands of great new businesses in the early development stages which just need a little capital and a little guidance to get off the ground. If every successful business would help one new, deserving start-up business, think about what a powerful chain of business success we would create! It is in this spirit that I am setting aside a portion of the proceeds of my book sales to help establish the next great start-up business, or help a business that has recently been started and could use a boost in order to really get off the ground. If that is your business, then please send me your business plan and enter the contest.

You may submit a business plan whether or not your company has been formally launched.

Mail to: Rebecca Matthias
MothersWork
P.O. Box 1829
Philadelphia, PA 19105

Your business plan should contain at least the following:

- Your short résumé of experience, and other key employees (if any)
- Overview of your business and its history
- The market size and nature of your business
- The competition
- Your strategy for success in the market
- Product or service description
- Financial history and forecast (at least three years)

- Total capital requirements

Please supply, as well, the following basic information:

- Your name
- Your company's name
- Your business type
- Business address
- Telephone and fax
- E-mail
- Web site (optional)

Official Contest Rules

1. *One Prize:* Ms. Matthias will select, on the strength of the best overall business plan, the winning entry on or before July 1, 2000. The sole criterion for choosing the winning entry is her judgment of the success potential of the overall business plan, regardless of the race, creed, gender, and parental status of the founders. The winning entry will be awarded $10,000.00 to help get the winner's business off the ground. Should the winner so choose, Ms. Matthias is willing to serve as a mentor and advisor to the company for a period of at least one year. The winner will be notified by mail, and posted on the MothersWork Web site.

2. Entries must be received by Ms. Matthias no later than March 31, 2000.

3. The winner will be chosen by Ms. Matthias from completed entries received. Ms. Matthias's decision will be final. The winner will be notified on or about July 1, 2000, and will have thirty (30) days from the date of notice in which to accept the prize, or an alternate winner will be chosen. Ms. Matthias is not responsible for late, lost, or misdirected entries.

4. The winner may be required to execute an Affidavit of Eligibility and Promotional Release. Entering the contest constitutes permission for use of the winner's name, likeness, biographical data, and contest entry, for publicity and promotional purposes, with no additional compensation.

5. Employees of Random House, Inc., its subsidiaries and affiliates, and their immediate family members are not eligible to enter this contest. This contest is open to residents of the United States and Canada, excluding the Province of Quebec, who are eighteen years or older on the date of entry. Void wherever prohibited or restricted by law. All federal, state, and local regulations apply. Taxes, if any, are the winner's sole responsibility.

6. For the name of the winner, available after August 1, 2000, send a self-addressed, stamped envelope entirely separate from your entry to MOTHERSWORK BUSINESS PLAN CONTEST, Doubleday Marketing, 1540 Broadway, New York, New York 10036.